A Book of Poetry

BLACK
LIVES, LINES, & LYRICS

Lines, Lyrics, and Laments for
Black Life, Love, Loss, and Liberty

D.B. MAYS

FIRST EDITION

Pictures/SVG SILH
Book design by Pinnacle Designs

ISBN 978-1-7365814-0-7 (hardback)
ISBN 978-1-7365814-1-4 (paperback)
ISBN 978-1-7365814-0-7 (ebook)

www.authordbmays.com

INTERIOR &
BACK COVER KEY

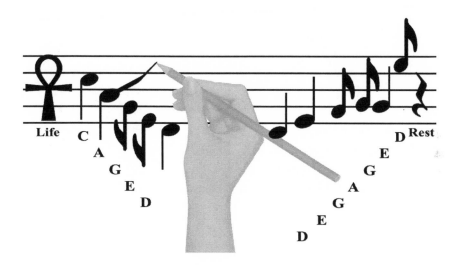

Ankh ☥: The Ankh is an Ancient Egyptian hieroglyphic for the word life. Ancient Egyptians also used the Ankh to symbolize the "cross of life" and to convey the spirit of God in all beings. Throughout the ages, the Ankh has come to mean many things in different cultures, but it is now most commonly used as a symbol of African identity. On this musical staff, the ankh is used in place of the treble, or G, clef to assign specific meaning to the notes and highlight themes.

Caged: The first five notes literally spell *caged* to illuminate the institutional, physical, and social confinement and oppression of Black people in America. The word *caged* is also used in reverence to the writer and activist who ignited my literary passion, Maya Angelou. Her poem, "Caged Bird," and book, *I Know Why the Caged Bird Sings*, were the first works to transform my life, and both inspired me to write.

Dégagéd (de-gah-zyeh): The last six notes literally spell *dégagéd*, which means free of constraint. In ballet, dégagé is a *movement*, not a position, where the working leg disengages from the supporting leg. I took the artistic liberty of adding *d* to the end, creating a suffix to signify how the Black Lives Matter movement inspired young people to disengage from their regular social routines to engage in social and political activism, using their individual and collective voices to protest racially motivated violence against Black people and exercising their social and civic responsibilities without fiscal and political support and, often, without leadership from the elders.

Quarter Rest Note 𝄽 : On a treble, or G, clef musical staff, the quarter rest note gives a period of silence that lasts for one beat. From the onset of the 21st Century, that's about how long Black Americans had to inhale and exhale before another racially motivated incident against blacks occurred. The quarter rest has one-fourth the value of a whole rest note, which is why I chose it – to symbolize how little value America places on Black life.

Poetry is music, and it provides the soundtrack of our lives. I used a music staff on the book cover to underscore the title and genre of the book. The Ankh symbolizes Black life, the notes are a lyrical representation of the highs and lows of the Black experience in the 21st Century, and the lines on the musical staff represent a time continuum wherein, decade after decade, we continually dégagé from the cages intended to confine us.

DEDICATION

This book is dedicated to Black people, with love,
and to everyone who used their voice, body, platform,
or other to proclaim that Black Lives Matter and
to stand against racial violence, racial inequality, and police brutality.

CONTENTS

EPIGRAPH

"I am overwhelmed by the grace and persistence of my people."

— Maya Angelou

"My writing has been largely concerned with the depicting of [Black] life in America."

— Langston Hughes

"If there's a book that you want to read, but it hasn't been written yet, then you must write it."

— Toni Morrison

"I aim to convey, through lines and verse, the Black experience as it is today so that the generations who come after us have a lyrical but accurate account of how we contended with racial and social injustice and violence during our lifetime. In essence, I write to promote the reverence Black people deserve for our resilience, beauty, and humanity."

— D.B. Mays

PREFACE

I don't need a social-struggle meter stick to measure which era in American history was harder for Black people. All withstanding, I believe that the 21st Century has been especially difficult on Black people of all ages, genders, religions, and socioeconomic backgrounds. And, someday, years from now, people, especially Black people, will need an account of this period in our lives. I think, now, more than ever, that our 21st Century racial struggles and our individual and collective determination to confront racism with uncompromising courage and resolve made us all appreciate Blackness just a little more than we ever did before. At the time I began writing this book in June 2020, America was still tiptoeing around having an honest discussion about what it really means to exist while Black in this country. In conversations on and offline, I continually found myself saying, "all lives can't matter if Black lives don't matter" and explaining why the demand for equality and equity isn't radical. I was so exhausted from constantly explaining how and why America's incongruous and duplicitous institutions, systems, and national ideals, symbols and documents are not an accurate reflection of Black life and experiences in this country that I decided to write about it. I thought, *'I don't know if others are writing about it, too, but there is room for more than one voice, one experience, and one portrayal of Black lives, lines, and lyrics.'*

With the literary influences and voices of my childhood, college, and adult years continually converging and disconnecting as I wrote, it was difficult for me to separate my multiple writing personalities and styles to choose one for this book. So, I didn't. Instead, I divided the book into three parts to better organize my thoughts, to maintain control of the central themes and underlying narratives, and to focus on one writing energy at a time. The poems in "Part I: Black Lyrics" are my musings and meditations on a variety of Black experiences and topics. The poems in this section flowed more naturally from me than those in the other sections, but there were a few that I had to revisit over and over, even as my publication deadline loomed. "Part II: Black Lives," which specifically focuses on police brutality and racial violence, was a labor of love that challenged me in ways I had not anticipated as I struggled to give a creative, poetic account of every life lost; balancing my artistic freedom with real-life people and events proved to difficult. The final part, "Black Lines," was supposed to be fun and light, affording me an opportunity to tap into my rap, or Hip Hop, ego. My initial goal was to include anywhere between five and eight lyrics and had a long list of working titles and notes, but I would struggle with Part III most because I wrote it last, after having exhausted myself on the depth and breadth of Part II. By the time I found my way to Part III, my mind and fingers were so bent out of shape that I had to tuck away many of my ideas for a second edition or poetry collection.

An avid reader, I reflected on the wisdom flowers I'd gathered reading the autobiographies and biographies of highly successful and acclaimed writers, and I forgave myself for not having the fuel left to write all the lyrics I intended to write for Part III. If the lyric poem wouldn't readily accept my invitation, I wasn't going to force it to write itself. While I have many writing heroes and heroines of all races and backgrounds who have fueled my love for literature and writing, none have been more influential in my development as a writer, educator, and mother than Black writers and, even they, vary in ideology, style, and purpose. "A Soliloquy to the Storytellers" is written in deference to a few of my Black literary heroes and heroines. The excerpt below, I think, best captures their individual and collective influence on this work. It also provides more insight about the *why* behind this writing. In re-reading their poetry and quotes, I heard their voices often as I wrote, and I thank them for speaking to me when I needed them.

> While *Their Eyes Were Watching God*, I was watching
> the TV and video streams, enraged by what was
> happening to people who look like you and me.
> Queen Mother Zora Neale Hurston, these poems are my
> *Dust Tracks on a Road* because this 21st Century time of
> *Mules and Men* and all the events therein must be told.
> You moved me to write this collection of poetry
> because *Every Tongue Got to Confess*
> the mess that is happening here; thus, as a
> budding poetess, I use my pen, I do my best
> to chronicle America's crimes against Black
> humanity, truths she tries to suppress.
> She has shoved so many lies down our throats,
> the country chokes and bursts its britches.

Exploiting our Black magic, her three branches
of government are like *Three Witches* –
one beguiles, one lies, and one deceives. Wait,
I'm describing the same damn thing.

One of the literary talents that I most appreciate about Harlem Renaissance writers, like Zora Neale Hurston, is that they, through their prose and poetry, creatively convey the cultural and political context of the literature so that the reader leaves each read enlightened about life during that period of time. I think I achieved this in Part II; if not, I know that I made a valiant effort. This epitaph precedes the poems in "Black Lives," a signal to the reader that the section has changed and that there is a shift in topic and themes. This poem is about as light and short as it gets for "Black Lives," understandably so considering the gravity of the experiences.

I am my brothers and sisters' keeper,
and for you, my brothers and sisters, I speak
through these lowly lines of poetry
to reverently record your collective release
from racial violence, injustice, and police brutality,
and, most importantly, to elevate your memories.

While I did manage to write and include a few bars in "Part III: Black Lines," please don't ever expect or request for me to perform them. I am a writer, not a lyricist. Even the statement *I am a writer* unnerves and excites me. This is my first professional writing effort; hence, my struggle with Part III. Admittedly, I did not write this book through from June until the publication date. I was forced to take a few hiatuses along the way because life wouldn't have it any other way.

Ultimately, this book was written *about Black people, for Black people,* and *to Black people,* but *it is also, an open and standing invitation to non-Black people* to get to know us Black people better: *all of us.* Black people are not monolithic, not as individuals or as a whole. That said, I wrote about the collective Black experience from the perspective of a Black American, Bahamian, and Black Native woman whose own lived experiences within the context of each of those spaces give shape to each poem. Even my perspective isn't the Black perspective. It's simply one perspective of many.

My goal, and I hope I accomplished it, was to treat our varied Black experiences with honesty and dignity. There will be some poems you love, like, and dislike. There will be others that will make you think, laugh, cry, frustrated, or angry. There will be some topics that you appreciate and others that you don't care for at all or you'd rather not address. I accept whatever range of emotions and experiences that you have with *Black Lives, Lines, and Lyrics* and truly want you to share them with me and other readers on Facebook and Instagram @ authordbmays. Thank you for supporting my work!

INTRODUCTION

As I began writing, I could feel the eloquence and cultural aesthetics of the Harlem Renaissance writers, the bold, fresh voices of contemporary authors, and the rhythm and flow of Hip Hop, soul, and pop artists of the 20th and early 21st Centuries, all of whom, at some point on my writing trajectory, informed my development and direction.

Thus, "Part I: Black Lyrics" provides a poetic perspective of living while Black in the 21ˢᵗ Century. These rhythmical reflections illuminate Black experiences with racial and social injustice, weaving culture into my poems like the Harlem Renaissance writers I admire.

"Part II: Black Lives" is a lyrical account of the lives lost to police brutality and racial violence. As poetry is neither fiction nor nonfiction, many of "Black Live's" poems are based on actual historical events. To provide context, the facts were included where necessary to include them – people, places, events, and outcomes, and if reported in multiple reputable sources. The Bibliography lists those sources. Other times I took creative liberties, and when doing so, I omitted names and places or created my own because the who or where embodies a prevailing idea, trait, or flaw in American society. Most of all, Part II aims to provide an honest portrayal of America's, in particular Black America's, really dark experiences. There was no way around it but through it. Sometimes you have to tell the whole damn truth no matter how ugly and painful it may be. America needs to smell and sit in her own feces for a while and walk around and let the world see her stained rear end and cover its nose at the stench of her democracy.

"Part III: Black Lines" is a poetic perspective of living while Black in the 21ˢᵗ Century. There is no central theme, just topics I wanted to address. My love and reverence for rap music, or Hip Hop, compelled me to drop a few bars and lines about the experiences of our time. Rap is a form of poetry and can be found in at least three subgenres of poetry: lyric (nearly every Hip Hop artist), narrative (think Tupac Shakur, Biggie, Jay Z), and dramatic poetry (think Biggie Smalls and a few of Jay Z and Beyonce's rap duets). I'm still getting my fingertips wet, so I stuck with rap lyrics, although I love rap narratives best.

For educators, especially English teachers, you'll find that I kept it pretty PG for ages 14+ so that you can use the text in its entirety if you are looking for a culturally relevant text. There are few expletives in three or four poems because they simply help to convey the speaker's tone and feelings, or they are direct quotes from human subjects in the poems. Still, even the canonized works include more expletives than this book does. When we teach poetry, we often focus on speaker, theme, tone, structure, style, form, and verse. You'll find that I used a variety of poetic forms and verse structures in this book, but more than anything, you'll see that the verses flow with my thoughts, often with little regard for rhyme and meter. I am rebellious in my style in that, it's my style. If I followed convention it is purely happenstance. If I failed to follow convention, it's because my virtual pen wouldn't permit it. For example, I intentionally do not capitalize *confederate* anywhere in this book because there is nothing *pro* about this noun, and I intentionally italicize titles of songs and many quoted statements when in verse instead of enclosing them in quotation marks. I thought the quotation marks were too distracting. While you might select this book or poems from the book to teach a contemporary poetry or women's lit unit, you might also use this text as an anchor for conventions, perhaps correction exercises. Your students are free to send me their critiques ☺!

I hope that secondary and higher ed English and Social Studies and Social Science instructors will use this work as an anchor or a supplementary text in a course or an interdisciplinary unit. I am working on a teaching guide and intend to have it published on my website by August 2021. For all teachers, white supremacy, racism, discrimination are real issues in our country that affect every aspect of our society, including the classroom. You can use this book to promote tolerance, stimulate thoughtful discussion, and more. I look forward to your discussions and questions about this work.

To all readers, I hope this book will serve as a conversation starter and an inspiration or call to action in your homes, communities, workplaces, and more about the Black experience, racial violence, and police brutality in this country. Most of all, I hope you enjoy reading this book, recommend it to others, and follow my social media pages @authordbmays. Thanks, again, for your purchase and support!

PART I

BLACK LYRICS

Musings and Meditations

BLACK DIAMONDS

for the ancestors

Black gemstones pillaged from Mother Earth, mined from Kemet,
crystallized into rare gems under centuries of pressure.
Yet, clarity remains pure under the brutal heat of history
and the alluvial mining along the coastlines of Black beaches.
Whitewashing while extracting Nubian gems from sable sands,
twelve million carats separated from the soil of Black lands.

Pipe mining Black diamonds from the canals of the Earth,
quarrying obscure jewels submerged in Her womb,
delivering gems to screening plantations, ghettos, schools, and prisons
to be efficiently processed, so they are conflict-free.
Gems cut too deep to diminish the light and detract from their beauty,
continually altering the clarity, cut, color, and coarse, shaping
Black diamonds into whatever they desire them to be.

Benumbed for ages. Woke, no longer asleep, excavating the
annals of history,
but the archives are dry like the river from decades of erosion
and whitewashed histories.
Still, sifting through plundered powder for Nubian surnames
that rose and fell with the tides along foreign shores,
swept from the shoreline and out to sea, adrift in the currents,
still brilliant and resilient, Black diamond gravel emerges in the
shallow seabed.

Though scattered and fractured over billions of years,
Indestructible are Black diamonds, forged in courage and strength,
weathered and battered, even now, Black is so radiant because the
gems are ideal.
Brilliant, sparkling, reflections glimmering impressively in the
dimmest light and under the darkest skies,
luminously shining in their refracted light, fire burning bright
through prisms of time, though it has been a difficult journey.

So extraordinary and rare that few subsist.
Indomitable, invincible, the most precious of stones,
symbol of love situated splendidly upon the vena amoris.
No two are the same, Black diamonds are uniquely their own.
Sparkle, Black diamonds. Keep shining!

A SOLILOQUY
TO THE STORYTELLERS

for the Black writers who capture and convey our stories so eloquently,
I dedicate this poem, in memory, to those who inspired me most

My wings thrashing wildly against the bars, bruised
and broken, I was concussed and confused.
I thought I would never fly away, would only know hurt, and so,
continually devalued my worth. Oh, to be a "Caged Bird," struggling
to find release from confinement without the tools to do it.
Queen Mother Maya Angelou, you showed me how
to use words to give voice to my truth,
and reading your words, I learned that I was not the first to entomb my hurt.
My eyes devoured every page, consuming and digesting
the experiences of my newfound sage,
who told me to use my hands to open my mouth,
and effortlessly, the words tumbled out.
Vomiting all the sorrow, fear, and pain, poetically,
I found hope and joy as I sang.
I cannot hold a tune or note, but *I Know Why the Caged Bird Sings*, I wrote.

It's been a long four years, and we've decided that we're tired of being tired.
So, we *Gather Together in [Your] Name*, dancing to your poetry
that has us *Singin and Swingin and Getting Merry Like Christmas*.
Exhausted, I wet my parched throat with *A Cool Drink of Water 'Fore I Diiie*
and prepare a feast for my guests. We dine on *Great Food All Day Long*
while debating the magnitude of our individual and collective struggles
and whether we would change anything in our past or present lives.
After some reflection, I realize that
I *Wouldn't Take Nothing for My Journey Now*.

D.B. MAYS

A wanderer in this wasted land, *Life Doesn't Frighten* me anymore,
but my feet are weary, and my soul is blue.
Still, your stories get me through, reminding me that
All God's Children Need Traveling Shoes.
Every time I reach a mile marker on my journey,
my *Soul Looks Back in Wonder* if you know
how many lives you've impacted,
how many women you've inspired
what you did for me, a little Black girl from Liberty
City and from *The Tree of Anglee.*

There is a young poetess, her name is Amanda;
she embodies your spirit and your grit,
like you, "I love to see a young girl go out and grab
the world by the lapels" and take hold of it.
Her poem, "The Hill We Climb," stirred the nation
much like "On the Pulse of Morning."
Surely, her *Song Flung Up to Heaven* and made your spirit dance in delight.
She is a *Phenomenal Woman*, like you, like me,
and like so many other *Black Pearls*
whom you've helped to harvest and cultivate
through your prolific prose and poetry.
And, understandably so, because you knew the
Heart of a Woman better than most,
and could convey it so well.

Queen Mother, in the midst of the rainstorms, *Still I Rise.*
When the rains have passed, and the sun comes out,
I search for you, my *Rainbow in the Cloud,*
striving with every line and verse I write, to grow
in the *Wisdom and Spirit of Maya Angelou.*

Queen Mother Toni Morrison,
we're still *Race-Ing Justice, En-Gendering Power* and, even in this late hour,
the hands move on the clock, but the time doesn't
change, everything remains the same.

Is it *The Mirror or the Glass*; is justice a fable? In
this country, it seems two-wayed.
What Moves at the Margin, do we sing, march, or vote – what works?
I have these *Conversations with [you]* in my head,
asking what I should do with all this hurt
and how to approach Part II of this book which
may be considered, at its best and worst,
a *Mouth Full of Blood* trying to balance *Goodness and the Literary Imagination,*
or a 21st Century assessment of *The Measure of Our
Lives* and a gift for the next generation.
They may *Burn This Book* someday because it
unapologetically addresses, with some cynicism,
the true *Origin of Others* – we know who the others are – and modern racism,
if there is such a thing. Queen Mother, does bigotry
modernize itself, do biases evolve?
I search for the answers while *Playing in the Dark*, and
often, wonder why I bother playing at all.

While *Their Eyes Were Watching God*, I was watching the TV and video streams,
enraged by what was happening to people who look like you and me.
Queen Mother Zora Neale Hurston, these poems are my *Dust Tracks on a Road*
because this 21st Century time of *Mules and Men*
and all the events therein must be told.
You moved me to write this collection of poetry
because *Every Tongue Got to Confess*
the mess that is happening here; thus, as a budding
poetess, I use my pen, I do my best
to chronicle America's crimes against Black
humanity, truths she tries to suppress.
She has shoved so many lies down our throats, the
country chokes and bursts its britches.
Exploiting our Black magic, her three branches of
government are like *Three Witches* –
one beguiles, one lies, and one deceives. Wait,
I'm describing the same damn thing.

Together, they stew a witch's brew, serving *Lies
and Other Tall Tales* to you and me.
That's why I am convinced that our people will
never be treated equally or have equity.
Sometimes I feel like *Seraph on the Suwanee*, in
search of a love that will never be.

Queen Mother Nikki Giovanni,
you gave me permission to have a *Black Talk* about *Black Feeling*,
absent *Black Judgment*, because our people need upliftment and healing.
Thus, some poems are like *Cotton Candy on a Rainy Day*,
while others are *Blues for All the Changes*.
Thank you for giving me the freedom to use this pen
to elevate *Those Who Ride the Night Winds*.

One Day When I Was Lost, I started writing because I had a lot to say.
Then I thought, who is going to want to read this
book when *Nobody Knows My Name*.
Sir James Baldwin, there was a time when no one knew yours either.
True to your convictions, you never let namelessness, or anything, deter
your literary course or alter your voice – you were a true literary leader.
You gave me the courage to have *A Dialogue,* unabridged, with the people.
Because *The Devil Finds Work* in idle minds, and I was so enraged,
I thought, I better put this pen to paper and give this *Rap on Race*.
For our fallen *Native Sons* and daughters,
I provide *The Evidence of Things Not Seen*
so that their lives aren't reduced to hashtags and chalk
marks, having *No Name in the Street*.

Queen Mother Alice Walker, the writer of my
college years, your prose and poetry
literally brought me to tears.
Revolutionary: Petunias and Other Poems inspired
me to write this book of poetry,
and one can only hope that it be received as a nod to your artistic creativity.

Like *Meridian*, I found it difficult to balance my support of the movement
with my personal struggles, but through activism
literature, I discovered I could do it.

While I was *In Search of Our Mothers' Gardens*, the journey was an arduous one.
In reconnecting with *The Temple of My Familiar*, I nearly became undone
because revisiting the historical atrocities inflicted
on Black people in this country
made it difficult to write without rage in my spirit and malice in my heart.
But in re-reading "Expect Nothing" and "We Alone," I came full circle,
and found beauty, again, in our humanity, relearning
to appreciate *The Color Purple*.
I hope my readers will be able to do the same and bear the uncomfortable parts,
because much like your pieces, my literary shards leave painful *Warrior Marks*.
So much so that I abandoned this work many times;
anti-Blackness is agonizing.
Every time I saw another Black person murdered on TV by the police,
I would say this is our antebellum, Jim Crow, and Civil Rights eras,
and I hope there are writers putting all the people, places, and events together
into artistic expressions that convey their perspective on what has occurred
during this "New Black Movement" in a way that the Black experience deserves.
Wait, who really determines that? Any Black lived experience and Black voice,
certainly, has the right to be heard in oral, sung, visual, and written words.

That's when I realized that *We Are the Ones We've Been Waiting For*
and that my poems may be an *Inner Light in A Time of Darkness* or more
for Black people, about Black people, and to
uplift Black people; notwithstanding,
this book is also an invitation to non-Black people
to gain insight, understanding,
and appreciation for our Blackness and what it
means to be Black in this century.
Maybe, they, too, were at a loss for words, like me,
seeing the lynching of human beings.

In *Gathering Flowers Under Fire*, I was *Overcoming Speechlessness,* in part,
because I was using lines and verse to say, *Now is the Time to Open Your Heart.*
Queen Mother Alice Walker, sometimes,
The Way Forward is With A Broken Heart.
You were right – *Anything We Love Can Be Saved,* but I must do my part.
I do love Blackness, the Black experience, the way we struggle and overcome.
Even when I didn't want to write, Queen Mother,
A Poem Traveled Down My Arm,
moving from my upper limb, extending to my elbow,
then wrist, and nestling at its crook
until it found its way to my fingertips,
onto the keyboard, and, finally, into this book.

Sir Langston Hughes, you are, indeed, one of my greatest literary heroes.
Like you, "I, Too," frequently shift back to Black
and away from *The Ways of White Folks.*
In Part II, I struggle to balance *The Weary Blues* with *Dear Lovely Death*
because the fatalities I write about were not lovely and often left me bereft.
Like you achieved with *The Panther and the Lash: Poems of Our Times,*
I pray I commemorate the modern Black experience well with these lines.
And if some feel that I have not, I'll be fine because appreciation
for literary works often increases with time.

"I, Too," am waiting on equality, but I think it's a fable; for us, it doesn't exist.
And, thus, I no longer want a seat at the table,
at least, not a table built like this.
When re-reading *Let America Be America Again,*
I was more than a little incensed.
I do not believe it a coincidence that your poem
was the premise of a presidential mantra.
In it, you remind us that there is no period in
American history that was ever great for us.
The last line of the poem is what we should keep in mind – it really tells it all.
If America is to BE America, it must fall;
we must tear it down, and rebuild it all.

We can't till the soil of democracy and justice
because *Freedom's Plow* is broken, sir,
and I thought you should know.
America is on a *One-Way Ticket* to hell, and the train is moving too slow.

In Memory
of the Black writers who passed in 2020 and 2021

Eric Jerome Dickey, Black Contemporary Fiction

Grace F Edwards, Cozy Mystery Series

Bryan Monroe, Journalist

Roscoe Nance, Sportswriter

Barbara Neely, <u>Blanche White</u> Mystery Series

Jas Waters, <u>This is Us</u> TV Series

They are listed in alphabetical order by last name, along with their literary/writing genres. Please forgive any omissions. Charge it to my head, not my heart.

AMERIKKKA

A-mer-i-ka
A mirror KKK
A reflection of her unsightly visage,
beautiful photoshopped exterior,
ugly interior but sits superior
to her sister lands,
the whore that she is.
Her derrière bears the skid marks
she tried to leave on Skidrow.
The whore that she is,
penetrated by prejudicial phallicism –
oops, fallacies, between her chaffed thighs.
Toxic milk spills from her teats
providing poisonous sustenance to her
entitled, bastard daughters and sons,
bequeathing them a false sense of superiority.
Still, she snubs her snout at her sister lands
while wiping white residue from her upturned nose,
inhaling so much of that wicked white girl, she overdosed.

THE GREAT MASQUERADE

an ode to Paul Laurence Dunbar

"How is it now?"
Master Dunbar, it's pretty much the same,
America has relatively remained unchanged.
We're four centuries in, and we still aren't free.
While we wear the mask, it's troubling me,
And I've been thinking on it for quite a while.
"Yeah, what's that, child?" Well, it's not us,
     but they who beguile.
It's those who govern, preach, police, and teach;
No, the great masqueraders aren't you and me.

They wear the mask that grins and lies,
Promoting America as the land of apple pie
Where white picket fences sit below blue skies,
Where they live and work in full disguise
And shield their racism behind smiling eyes, while
     They wear the mask.

They wear the mask that grins and lies,
Teaching black children whom they despise,
Corrupting young souls and crippling young minds,
Failing and suspending our students at record highs, while
     They wear the mask.

They wear the mask that grins and lies,
From their pulpits they preach of the Most High
Pale palms and faces pointed earnestly toward the sky
And using biblical scriptures to spread more lies, while
     They wear the mask.

They wear the mask that grins and lies,
Because of our hue, they criminalize us and justify
Beating us bloody, kneeing necks, and shooting us until we die
Hiding behind their silver badges and blue disguise, while
　　　They wear the mask.

They wear the mask that grins and lies,
From the White House to the legislative aisles,
Passing laws and judgements that oppress our lives,
Stripping away and repressing our rights, while
　　　They wear the mask.

What's that Master Teacher?
Yes, we must do our best
Because we know that you expect nothing less.
For your sacrifices, we rise to the task, while
　　　We wear the mask.

It takes so much energy to exert
Our faux faces and maintain our self-worth,
To shield our pain and hide our hurt,
But we dare not show them otherwise.
So, we grin and lie and compromise, while
　　　We wear the mask

Oh, but her mask cracks beneath her grins and lies,
The weight of it all will be our collective demise.
Behind her stars and stripes and spangled disguise,
Riots and insurrection arise, while
　　　She wears the mask.

No, let the world see America as we know her to be
A democratic tease who works the streets
Cloaked in a myriad of prejudicial subtleties.
Nay, let the world see her and all her inhumanity –
Why should we wear the mask?

BLACKTIVITY

Nobody paints like God.

The most colorful creations are His most precious works –
From the mahogany mounds of Mother Earth
To the ebony silk of the evening sky,
Bespattered with brilliant stars shining bright
And suspended over the splendid, sable sea.
Though all His works are wondrous beauties,
God's greatest paintings are of you and me.
From rich chocolate to chestnut brown,
Buttery beige to deep ebony,
Terra-cotta cocoa to coffee ground,
Russet cinnamon to rich mahogany.
Unquestionably, his most impressive palette includes you and me.
We're the most vibrant creations of the human rainbow,
With each stroke of His sun, our melanin glows.
Highly valued, coveted, and appraised,
Provenance validated, a remarkable collection of black,
His signature, texture, and layering intact.
Over the canvases of time, a premium price is paid
For His master drawings and most treasured antiquities.

Indeed, God's greatest paintings are of you and me.

STUNNING

for our Black daughters

Why you tryin' to look like 'dem?
Don't 'cha know from where yo' hips grow,
Why 'dey sway to and fro'
From west to east
Hind rise like yeast?
Melanin rich and honeyed, butter brown syrupy
'Da blacker the berry, the sweeter the sweet.
Girl, all hues of the ebony rainbow shine
Our rind so rare, age like fine wine
Lips plump like cherries ready to be picked.
Dey spend all kind of money tryin' to look like 'dis,
But do all that 'dey can
To make ya' feel less than.
Puttin' up 'dem white-right pictures
Sellin' 'dey likeness when you 'da fixture.
Yep, you really 'da center of the universe.
That's right, gurl, you were here first.
They come from you – now ain't 'dat da truth?
Still, you want 'ta be dem, and dey want 'ta be you.
Umph, now ain't 'dat da truth?
'Dey want to be you, pooh. 'Dey want to be you!
So, why you tryin' to look like 'dem
When you're so beautiful in the skin you're in.

MY LITTLE GIRL'S
COILS & CURLS

for my daughter whose hair is magical and beautiful and
for Ms. Charlotte who poured love and life into it

It's wash day so you groan,
but I cue the girl empowerment songs
because this regimen is at least three hours long
and we both have to remain strong.
I didn't inherit the hands or skills of our surname,
Breedlove, aka Madame CJ Walker, and that's a shame.
If I did, it would only take me half the time to tame this mane.

I begin with adding coconut oil and moisture to detangle the knots
Oh, I should have made an appointment with Ms. Charlotte at the shop!
Whew! Start at the roots, combing gently up the hair shaft to free the kinks,
Then wash tenderly but thoroughly over the kitchen sink.
Using warm water and shampoo that's sulfate free,
your afro hair absorbs the H2O, making it springy and spongy.

Rinse with warm water and deep condition, heavily coating the ends.
Under the dryer with a plastic cap, sit for 30, and then cold-water rinse.
Do a hot oil treatment to add moisture and elasticity,
under the dryer, sit a bit, then rinse, pat dry, and break to eat.
Part your thick mane in sections, moisturize with oils to enhance the shine,
and rub black castor oil, coconut oil, and shea butter
through your tresses and between the lines.

The hood in me can't help it, so I grab a toothbrush
to smooth your edges with gel.
I know you don't like it; you try to suppress sucking
your teeth, but my ears never fail.

My patience is thin, so, don't get popped with
this comb for your smellin' yourself.

As I struggle to style your hair in two afro puffs, you began to squirm.
"Mommy, please, pretty please, can I just get a perm?"
You want a relaxer so that your hair is always glossy and rests on your back,
but you must understand that the structure of your
hair is what makes it shiny and flat.
When it's pressed, the cuticles are smooth and closed;
so, it's straight and reflects better light.
When it's coiled and kinky, the cuticles are raised
so it looks a little bushy and dry.

No relaxer, nooo. I've told you that your natural curls will grow on you.
You'll learn to love the flexibility of your hair and, one day, others will, too.
We're finished, and I'm tired because for four hours I've been on my feet.
When I tell you to put on the satin bonnet, you think
it's to protect your hair when you sleep.
The truth is that if I have to do this again tomorrow,
I'm going to scream and weep.

One day comes, and you hop in the car, all bouncy, bright, and full of light.
I can tell you have a story to share, your eyes are twinkling with delight.
"Mommy, they asked, 'How do you go from straight to coils to curls to fro?'
They think it's magic or a weave, but I told them,
no, my hair can do just about anything.
I can wear braids or a weave or wear my hair flat,
in twists, coils, or an afro, if I please.
And I can add water and gel to make it curly or
wavy; my hair is a magical part of me."

"I know I asked for a perm way back when"
(like last week).
"You were right – natural hair is the trend again"
(when I told her so, she sucked her teeth).
I smile because sometimes I get it right,

but I'm struggling with this comb tonight.
Her coils and curls are tight, putting up a fight,
and I'm pulling and tugging with all my might.

Still, I love my little girl's coils and curls
because her head of afro hair is so diverse.
It's the most magnificent in the universe!
Sometimes her curls spiral, or they are loose or tight.
Either way her coils and curls adorn her crown just right.
Oh, my little girl's coils and curls are a beautiful sight!

THE SKIN YOU'RE IN

for my son, who is the color of dark roasted coffee

On the sixth day, God made man,
but ten hours later he created you.
5000 feet above sea level and nearest the Heavens,
He needed more time to cultivate your hue.
High in the Blue Mountains of Jamaica,
He single-blended the finest of coffee beans.
Grown in rich soil, rinsed in a continuous heavenly mist
until your blend of black was pristine.
Your brown given more time to deepen,
until the shade was perfectly whole.
Then He hand inspected the sheen of your shell,
leaving the residue to settle in your hull.
Admiring your smooth, unblemished texture,
He was pleased He had done so well.
He perfected a dark roasted, silky blend,
the richness and consistency of your color intact.
French pressed the grounds into the skin you're in,
producing a decadent cup of Black.

OUR BLACK LOVE

And so, it was written in the heavens above:
I had one wing until I met you –
Now, together, we have two.
We fly high into the sky,
pull down the night,
and wrap our love in the stars.
Together, we shine bright.
We are the light –
Our union changed the trajectory
of our respective and now connected families.
What once was you is now me, and we –
We are creating an enduring legacy
from our Black love.

OUR LOVE IS LIKE THE RIVERS

Our love is as ancient as the Nile,
overflowing long ago when our hearts gave way along the riverbank.
From its beginning, we connect and flow like Ethiopians,
enduring the length of time and ebb and flow of circumstance.
Our love is a perennial stream, the flood is constant in all seasons.
We weather the dust storms at love's basin, bask under the blue sun,
and then, delightfully, raft the waters and splash in our melanin,
creating and nourishing a new and advanced civilization
that is populated by people who descend from you and me.
Spanning eleven generations, such beauty from one stream,
a rising dynasty, our kingdoms are Kush, Egypt, and the Sudanese.
Thus, we rise, fall, and rise again, our realm stretching to the Mediterranean Sea
where our waters swell, spilling life into our
progenies so they prosper for posterity.
Our love flows like the River Nile, moving rapidly,
providing a lifeline to our legacy.

Our love is complex like the River Congo, sometimes
we go through thick rainforests,
crossing the same area twice; it requires an ocean of understanding from us both
to find our way over and through it because it is a channel
that we can't cross if the Atlantic is dragged between us.
We often exhaust ourselves from love's undercurrents,
but right before the avalanche and before we are completely spent,
we drain its contaminants and release compassion and mercy into love's basin.
Though the rapids of our love are high and turbulent at times, the flow is fast,
so, we rush past the Gates of Hell, eventually,
drifting in the steady stream of love,
the kind that calms and soothes and wraps itself around us like healing waters.
We like it here, so we steer clear of the low-lying places, rocky walls, and falls.

Like the Congo, we experience rainy season year-
round, but our love does not overwhelm;
it finds refuge in its side streams, tributaries of
respite that replenish our depleted waters.
Our love surges and gains strength from the passionate
torrents of the Congo and Tanzania,
quiets and steadies itself on the affirming and
familiar streams of Angola and Zambia.
The headstreams of our love feed our souls, spooning tenderness and friendship
and helping us digest the pressures of life with dollops of intimacy and joy.
Our love's course is unconventional, it moves
differently, creating its own model.
Like the Congo, the anatomy of our love is a
mystery, but it acts as one body, one soul.
Our waters swell, spilling life into our progenies
so they may prosper for posterity.
Our love is deep like the River Congo, impenetrable, too deep to be breached.

Our love is like the River Okavango, it's you and me,
we do not flow into another other sea.
Our love is like the River Niger, it bends, it's reciprocal,
what I give to you, you give to me.
Our love is like the River Zambezi that houses
Victoria falls, our love is a natural wonder –
it falls all around us, our love is the love that thunders.
Our love is like the river that swallows other rivers
– our love consumes other loves whole.

Our love flows like the rivers, streams link us from West to East.
Our love flows like the rivers, like the rivers, our love runs deep.

D.B. MAYS

COLOR ME BLACK

Lord, if I should die before I wake
Lord, promise me, on this very day
That I won't return no pale face.
'Cuz I like the cool, must have the swag,
Be the number one hustler who gets the bag.
Hell, I like being the best they ever had.

So, please bring me back the darkest hue,
Dip me in chocolate 'cuz I gotta' be smooth.
Lace me in ebony, drape me in jewels –
Black diamonds, black pearls, onyx, and black sapphire.
Bring me back the smoke that lingers long after a fire –
Ungelded black stallion with a beautiful mare to farm the foals I'll sire.

Just bake me black beneath the sun, Most High.
Bring me back a Blackbird, so I'll have the sight
And be the most knowledgeable of all birds in flight.

Make me black coal, 'cuz I bring the heat.
If I must be water, make me the Black Sea –
Water anoxic, layers so deep, asphyxiate
any explorer trying to navigate me.

Lord, if I die, and I must come back,
Please, Lord please, color me Black!

ERASED

Falling,
plummeting,
sinking into obscurity over and over,
disappearing into ominous
shadows that engulf us
until all that is left are our silhouettes.

OF COLOR

Who am I? Who gets to decide?
How is it that I can choose to be any religion,
party, even a boy or girl,
but my ink is permanent when I enter this world?
On color I do not get to feel or choose,
so, every decade, I lose, I lose
because dark is less than white and blue
even when they change the classification of my hue
from Copper to N----- to Negro to Black
to Person of Color – I don't know what to do with that.

What does it mean to be "of" color?
Yeah, it really does make me wonder.
If they can assign a new label to me
to fit their new-age policies,
then I should be free to change me
to whatever color I feel or need me to be.

So, the next time I'm stopped by a cop,
I'm gonna tell him I'm white
and smile, chile, I'm gonna smile real wide.
When he shines his light,
I'm gonna say, "shine it bright
You'll see my white better in the light
Because I'm feelin' real white tonight."

BLACK FIST

Black Lives Matter doesn't mean this fist, but it does mean resist
when oppression and injustice are not up for discussion,
insurrections and protections when wrongs aren't corrected.
It means black is equal, inherits the same rights,
liberties, protections, and the pursuit of happiness as whites.

Black Lives Matter does mean this fist.
It means equity in healthcare, housing, and education,
living in our communities without provocation,
receiving a citation without persecution,
eradication of discrimination, prejudice, and bias in all institutions.

Black Lives Matter will never again mean this!
To tyranny and racism, we will no longer submit.
We will not cower to oppressive powers,
no longer be silent about government violence.
We will combat racially motivated violence against blacks.

This includes racist Kevins and Karens,
Politicians, judges, educators, and cops.
We will have justice; we will not stop!

HYPOCRISY ON THE HILL

Feet on pavement, legs moving forward, all in one direction,
Bodies bending over to rinse the faces of fallen friends
with cool milk and lend open hands,
and no one stops until every man, woman, and child reach the destination –
the White House where he is lurking and peeping from behind the curtains.
Mouths open in harmony, chanting, and demanding protection
against common foes – inhumaneness and inequity; in unity, they stand.

Had they proceeded as the Proud Boys and QAnon and planned insurrection,
perhaps the media and politicians would excuse the good citizens for being misled
by the U.S. Constitution, as written by the founding fathers, in its decree
"That all Men are created equal, that they are endowed by their Creator
with certain unalienable Rights, that among these are Life, Liberty ..."

Maybe the law would have stood aside and let the peaceful passersby
walk into the Oval office, rest their weary feet atop the President's desk,
leave a handwritten note expressing their frustration
and detailing their public decry,
remove classified files, urinate in the corridor, tour staff offices, and leave a mess
after snapping selfies with police and taking a souvenir, national relic, or two.

All would be justified because they were told a lie, right? Not because they presented
physical proof of Black men, women, and children, yes Black citizens, being abused
in a series of videos, images, and interviews showing
the darkest hues of the underrepresented
chased, beaten, kneed, choked, hanged, and killed
by officers of the law and vigilantes,
Black men crying out for their mothers, black sisters
pleading for the lives of their brothers,
Black grandmothers using their bodies to shield their
Black sons from the barrels of policemen's guns,

Black babies made to lie face down on hot concrete while
their Black mothers are harassed by police,
Black women stripped naked in their homes during
unlawful searches, robbed of their dignity,
or shot to death under no-knock entry, the consequential
cases of incompetence and mistaken
identity.

Oh, but if we believe the election was stolen, we
have the right to be and act irate,
storm the Hill, beat and kill police officers, threaten
elected officials, and destroy a public place.
Nooo, the government doesn't order police to gas
citizens who participate in mutinies!
Gas and rubber bullets are only for citizens who
demand Blacks be treated equally,
who want civic overseers, unjust laws, officers, and
officials to face public and legal scrutiny,
and not be allowed to threaten, falsely accuse, chase,
beat, knee, and kill Blacks with impunity.

Yeah, that kind of special treatment is reserved
for people like you and me, you see –
The harassment, beating, or murder of a Black
person isn't a valid reason for civil unrest.
Though we see it on live TV, an expert panel explains how and
why our fellow human is stripped of his life and liberty,
Cautions us to respond civilly and peacefully after we
witness someone in blue crush a man's chest,
Then tells us to wait for all the facts and offers sage
advice about the way we should protest.

But IF the election is *STOLEN*, we don't need to wait for the *FACTS*.
We can blame it on political ignorance and the common sense we lack,
and we can use our immoral elected officials and fake
news to excuse our *SEDITIOUS ACTS*.

BLACK LIVES MATTER, TOO

in appreciation for the Black Lives Matter Movement

BLACK LIVES MATTER, too, the same as YOU.
MY life holds the same value as YOURS –
I bleed the same blood, feel the same hurt,
Breathe the same air, walk the same Earth.

BLACK LIVES MATTER, too, the same as YOU.
I am not lesser; you are not greater.
You are not superior, I am not inferior
Though we may differ in our exterior.

BLACK LIVES MATTER, too, the same as YOU.
What matters to you, also matters to me
The right to pursue love, life, and liberty.
BLACK LIVES MATTER, TOO.

OH, WON'T YOU BE MY NEIGHBOR?

'Oh, here comes k; here we go again.
I can tell k's heated by the way k's rounding that bend.

Peace be still – Lord, give me the will
To maintain my composure, be even keel

To speak truth to light and be polite,
No one needs to get hurt tonight.

Woosah, I'm ready. Let me keep my tone steady,
Although k's the one coming in hot and heavy.'

"Hello, *neighbor*, how is your day –
Why do you insist on walking my way?

What transgression did I commit
To inspire your latest tyrannical fit?

What's that neighbor, what did you say?
You're policing the amenities for which I pay the HOA?

I'll swim in the pool whenever I choose,
Invite guests to use it, too, because I pay my dues.

Yes, this is my dog that I'm walking; she is on a leash,
But I'm on your side of the street, so you'll call the police?

I am having an open house, but you'll call the cops
When you know full well that I own this lot.

Oh, I don't belong here, but you believe that you do?
Give you my full name and credentials as proof

That I live here, work here, and pay bills here, too?
And if I refuse, what will you do?

Oh, you'll call the law and tell them that someone black
Does not belong where you are at?

You'll endanger my life, attempt to manipulate my fate
Because you're threatened by and feel superior to my race?

You don't recognize the irony in that – that
You're afraid of my shade but still believe you're better than black?

Who appointed you the neighborhood watchman, keeper of the gate?
Careful neighbor – you're violating my personal space.

I will exercise my 2nd amendment right and stand my ground,
Protect my person from karens, kevins, and dangers abound.

To avoid unnecessary bloodshed, cooler heads must prevail
Lest our local news recount a terrible tale

Of one neighbor's failed attempt to make a citizen's arrest
Who now lay slain from a fatal bullet wound to the chest.

No, this is not a threat, but it is a promise I'll keep
Should you attempt to bring bodily harm to me.

Let us retreat to our respective homes
For it is apparent that we can't ALL get along.

Oh, say 'good night,' neighbor because I bid you adieu.
It is unlikely that a connection will forge between us two.

Again, what transgression did I commit of late
To be the addressee of your anger and the beneficiary of your hate?

On this matter, I shall no longer belabor. Instead, I'll offer this reply,
"I wouldn't want you to be my, I don't need you to be my,
I don't want you to be my neighbor."

D.B. MAYS

THE BLACK BOOK: LESSONS YOU SHOULD KNOW

from Black parents to Black children

There are a few lessons we want you to know
Carry them in your backpack wherever you go
From grade to grade and class to class,
Make no missteps, there is no hall pass.
From Kindergarten, you're perceived a threat,
Temper tantrums make you an expendable misfit.
Be quiet, not loud, or you'll be labeled hostile,
And anything you do will be added to your permanent profile.

Don't get too excited or raise your voice in anger
Or make sudden movements, less you're perceived a danger.
Fidgeting and daydreaming will get you meds,
Deliberately misdiagnosed and placed in Special Ed.

Dear Black child, as you matriculate from K to 12,
Here are a few more lessons that will serve you well:
It's really important that you know how to act
If you want to succeed at learning while Black.
Eighty percent of teachers are overwhelmingly white;
No matter what you say or do, they'll always be right,
And some believe Black students are inconsequential;
Thus, they'll have low opinions about your potential.

So, you'll find it very difficult to get them to endorse
A rigorous program for you to pursue, of course.
They will not inform you that the classes you take
Usually inform your future path, position, and place.
Instead, they'll focus on how well you conform

To their prison-like rules and following the norms.
Don't offer unsolicited opinions; that's talking back –
White peers can press, but you're provoking while Black.

Your thoughts and ideas will be dismissed and undermined;
Expect to be unduly chastised and unfairly criminalized.
Everyday actions will garner unwanted attention,
And you're nearly four times more likely to get a suspension
For noncompliance and willful defiance
And minor infractions that are completely nonviolent.

If you graduate at the top of the class,
You can count on the white student that you surpass
To demand a recount because it could never be true
That you are the better of the two of you.
They'll recalculate GPAs, rewrite policy overnight
Until Black is number two and number one is white, right?

Child, learning doesn't cease at commencement.
When you leave the schoolhouse, these lessons are amended
To reflect my-Black-life-matters and I-want-to-live rules.
You know, the lessons to live by when you're not in school.
Black child, these rules will apply wherever you roam,
Could be the difference of you returning home whole.
Be mindful because this is real life; this is not pretend.
It's not a matter of if, but it's a matter of when.

How well you take heed and listen in
Might determine if we ever see you again.

You can't play with toy guns,
You can't run for fun,
You can't play in the park,
Or take a jog in the dark.
You can't play hide-and-go seek,

Or you'll get killed in these streets.
Don't put stuff in your pockets that can be misconceived
As a weapon you can use to harm or frighten the police.

Because you're Black, the police assume deceit.
Hence, you can't hide anything except for your teeth
Safely tucked inside your gums and behind your lips,
And don't you dare grin, less a cop loosen his grip
On that weapon he'll certainly have aimed at you
Because your Black life has no value to the men in blue.

When you get pulled over, have your papers ready;
Place both hands on the wheel and hold them steady.
Explain what you're about to do before you do it
And don't challenge the stop or ask him to prove it.
Just be calm, speak clearly, be respectful and polite.
Save the argument for the courtroom if you value your life.

The police will ask you questions, tell you to be a good sport.
Remember, anything you say can be used against you in court.
If you exit the vehicle, keep your hands up, palms unclenched and flat,
No sudden movements because you're a danger – you're Black.
Although you know you are innocent, do not protest,
And whatever you do, do not resist arrest.
They'll use anything you say or do to justify
Their malintent and rationale for ending your life.

Always film the police and make sure you are live
Because in the courtroom there is only his or her side.
Ask for your parents, an attorney, and your phone call
Get and give the officer's name, number, and precinct to all
And don't sign anything; make no confession.
If you remember nothing else, remember this lesson:
Comply, even if it hurts your heart and injures your pride.
Dear Black child, the most important thing is for you to come home alive.

BALLAD OF A BLACK PARENT

for Tangela, David (RIP David), and Parents of Murdered Children

Every time you leave our home, I don't know if you'll return
whole, broken, in pieces, harmed, emotionally terrorized, dead or alive.
That's why I live in a perpetual state of fear, wondering when it will be my turn
to receive that dreadful knock at the door, asking me if this is where you reside,
telling me that you have been arrested, harmed, kidnapped, or worst – killed,
asking me to identify you in the county line up,
missing persons board, or morgue,
taking me to the place where you were detained,
abducted, or your blood spilled,
and requesting that I provide information about you to complete their report.

The wail I release comes from so deep, it paralyzes
my vocal cords, and I cannot speak.
I'm gasping for air, breathless and restless, going
around circles searching for you.
I walk around in a daze – my subconscious tells
me that I'm awake, but I fell asleep
yesterday when they told me that you were gone,
when I learned that I can't undo
what happened to you, nor can I pretend that my
entire life didn't meet a tragic end
as did all the hopes and dreams I had for you, and
the memories in between, they seem
like fantasies that play out in my head, illusions of an imaginary life unfurled.
The reality is that I couldn't protect you from this hateful world that snuffs out
Black boys and girls.

D.B. MAYS

If God would grant me one more day with you, I'd tell you how I love you still,
spend time doing your favorite things, and then I'd prepare your favorite meal.
Come back to me, my love so that I may wrap
you in my warm embrace, lay your
weary head on my chest.
Let me hum your favorite lullaby, you know the
one I sang when you were a babe,
run my fingers through your coils, wipe the tears from your eyes, and remind
you that God loves you best,
and then hold your hand tightly as you journey onward and release it when you
finally arrive at Heaven's gate.

THE ROAD NOT TAKEN

for our Black sons, a nod to Robert Frost

Two paths diverge in our neighborhood,
And sorry, you cannot travel both
And be akin to your Caucasian counterpart, as you should.
But don't take his path, is that understood?
Or you'll find yourself confronted by an interlope.

Take the other, for it is safer there,
Although trekking perhaps the hazardous lane.
Still, be wary of your walk and what you wear;
Though your companion intends to meet you there,
Your journeys will not be quite the same.

And the trails before you equally lay
Albeit uneven when trodden black.
Oh, I hope you'll walk the first someday!
Devoid of roadblocks that'll surely come your way,
And absent the perils of living while Black.

I hope you'll remember this by and by
In all your travels this day and hence:
Two roads diverge in our neighborhood, and I –
I implore you to take the one we travel by,
Because it will make all the difference.

BLACK FATIGUE

We wear fatigue like prisoners of war
Camouflage our distress in gilded smiles
To mask the sorrows of yore
And conceal the aching from forlorn travails,
Weary from the physical exertion of keeping our disposition intact,
While suffering from the mental exhaustion of existing while Black
And cloaking ourselves in an amalgamation of faith, courage, and grit
Because that's what it takes to get through this, this sewage pit –
Yeah, that's what it takes – grit ... you got to have grit to do this
Day in, day out, over and over and over again
From sunup to sundown, we pretend ... yeah, we pretend.
Still, we get up and rise with each new dawn
And shake off yesterday's shit with a head nod and a yawn.

THE PRISONER
SPEAKS OF PRISONS

a literary nod to Langston Hughes, for our incarcerated Black fathers, mothers,
daughters, sons, sisters, and brothers, and all innocent, over-charged, or over-
sentenced Black people, especially Kalief Browder, the Jena Six, & Central Park Five

I've known prisons:
I've known prisons ancient as the Kemetian tombs and chattel slavery;
older than cotton and sugar cane plantations and the slave patrol; as
debilitating as education, economic, housing, and health inequities; and
as brutal as the Louisiana State Penitentiary and modern-day policing.

I've known prisons ancient as the myth of black
criminality that make Blackness weaponry.
And because of it, my body and soul are scarred from the chains of history.

My community, my people have been crippled,
victimized, and terrorized by prisons.

I was bounded by Pharoah in Egypt, though not
without modern-day controversies.
I was tethered on the trails that trekked me from one territory to the next.
I was shackled on the ships that carried me across the Atlantic into bondage.
I was held captive on the plantations that enslaved me for over 400 years.
I was restricted by the Black Codes enacted
immediately following my emancipation.

The Civil Rights Act of 1866 supposedly *granted* me *equal rights*
to *whites,* but the Black Codes limited my privilege and regulated
my movement and progress for the rest of my Black life.
A 13th Amendment loophole ensured my freedom with a contingency
for subsequent centuries, making it easier for the systems and
dominant race of society to criminalize me for anything.

Slavery and servitude would be illegal in all circumstances,
"except as punishment for crime."
This clause would look differently over the course of
history modernizing my confinement over time.

I was forced into the prison labor and convict
lease systems during Reconstruction.
I was locked up during Jim Crow until I could Freedom Ride no more.
I was jailed during the Civil Rights Movement,
after being hosed, bitten, and beaten.
I was incarcerated in the '70s when mass incarceration was on the rise under
Johnson and Nixon who criminalized Civil Rights
activism, classifying it as street crime.
I was imprisoned during the War on Drugs and under three-strike
laws, ensuring I'd serve longer sentences and 85% of my time.
Yeah, America is real, real *tough* on alleged Black crime.

I was booked in the local jail under pre-trial detention
because I did not have the money for bail.
I was handcuffed, convicted, and sentenced for misdemeanors
and lower offenses and forced to perform penal labor.
I was committed to psychiatric hospitals and other
facilities for living with a mental illness
or for having a psychiatric disability.
I was caged in the immigration detention centers for being
undocumented and having questionable citizenry.
I was detained in the public schools and sent to juvenile
corrections to get a head start on the pre-school to prison
pipeline for my so-called classroom crimes.

I was held in solitary confinement from the ages of 26 to 69. For
43 years, 23 hours a day, I was in an isolated cell; the only prisoner
in American history isolated for most of my prison time.

I was confined since *1953 at age 15* and *released* in 2021 *when I*
was 82 years old, nearly *70 years* too late, making me the oldest
juvenile to serve a full life sentence in these United States.

I've known prisons:
Biased, imbalanced, unjust, and incapacitating prisons.
Prejudiced, partial, pointless, and paralyzing prisons.

I've known prisons ancient as the myth of black
criminality that make Blackness weaponry.
And because of it, my body and soul are scarred from the chains of history.

My community, my people have been crippled,
victimized, and terrorized by prisons.

VOTING WHILE BLACK

for the people who organize registration drives,
count ballots, and protect voters' rights

I pack my card, ID, and lucky pen; I'm on my way to the polling place again.
Yesterday I waited in line for hours and then, decided to leave at ten past ten.
Every election it's the same thing, change my precinct, can't find my name
Make me play the waiting game, ask me to return later for more of the same.

Nearly one week later, I have a little luck,
But when I get to the ballot box, I get a little stuck.
I read the ballot from top to bottom, left to right, and front to back,
But I see there are only two or three candidates who are Black.

No exaggeration, it's just a fact,
And I'm not sure what to do about that.

I guess I'll choose the lesser of two evils
Though no party has committed to doing anything for my people.
Still, they flood my phone with texts and calls, but I can't be relentless?
When I make demands, I'm ridiculed, ignored, and dismissed.

But I must vote – at least that's what they say,
So, I cast my ballot anyway and pray.

BREAKING BLACK NEWS: READ, SEE, HEAR ALL ABOUT IT!

for the Black journalists who fight to treat our people and stories with dignity

A Black body lies writhing, heartbeat slowing, blood pouring in the street,
These constant, traumatizing pictorials are distressing to me,
But cameras keep rolling, no obscuring the horror and terror aired,
Reprehensible indiscretions – some moments in life aren't meant to be shared.

Still, the person's dignity, memory, and family aren't spared,
Perpetuating images of black men, women, and children defiled,
Repeatedly flashing the trauma of the black man, woman, and child.
Yet, when white people murder or are murdered, the networks blur their profile.

In fact, the incident itself is never aired because it is deemed *"too graphic"*
For viewers to see *white people* involved in anything tragic.
Yeah, the media desensitize how black people are treated, normalize black pain
And manipulate the discussion of how Black people protest for change.

Depictions of police, their guns pressing against the temples of Black children,
Kicking, kneeing, beating, brutalizing, and shooting Black women and men.
Onlookers and audiences no longer horrified by the loss of Black lives
And have little to no empathy for the Black parents,
spouses, and children left behind.

Irreputable media manipulating facts and misrepresenting truths,
Belittling Black families of victims during detached interviews,
Criminalizing victims, and then biasedly presiding over their public trials,
Assassinated by the media, cunningly composing narratives to beguile.

PORTLAND TO PAPUA

for the Black Lives Matter protestors around the globe

The world stood in solidarity
as Earth cried out for and called out to
her Black daughters and sons
who, from all limbs of their Mother's tree,
joined together in unity
against racism, their common enemy.
From Portland to Papua New Guinea,
a sea of Black faces, joined by all races,
protested racial inequality and police brutality.

Wake up, Mother said, you are Black,
no matter your culture, belief, or creed,
Look at the dark skin you're in,
the world devalues your melanin.
So, stand together or perish in isolation.

And they heard, stood, and found courage
to take up the fight, marching, and squaring off
with police, getting beaten in the streets,
toppling statues to the ground,
like Washington, Jackson, Jefferson,
Colston, Milligan, and Leopold
and many other colonists and racists of old.

The live video of police kneeing George Floyd
to death for 8 minutes and 46 seconds
sparked a global awakening and reckoning
unlike anything the Earth had dreamed
when she corralled her Ebony to Ivory offspring.

And they moved their feet
and took to the streets in summer heat
to say the names of their slain brothers and sisters in distant lands.
In America, from Louisville to Minnesota to lily white Portland,
they chanted "#SayHerName, Breonna!" and for George, "I Can't Breathe!"
In Belgium, it was justice for Madwa, Adil, and Mehdi.
They marched in Columbia for Anderson Arboleda in Puerto Tejada
In France, they flooded the streets for Traoré, Adama,
who, like George Floyd, died in police custody,
he, too, was choked, couldn't breathe but in another country.
In Kenya, they demanded justice for the unnamed fifteen,
for Obby Kogoya in Indonesia, and for Solomon Teka in Tel Aviv.
In South Africa, they took to the streets
for 16-year-old, Nathaniel Julies who had a disability.
They chanted "Justice for Belly Mujinga!" in the UK,
The protests spread to Rio de Janeiro, Syria, Seoul, and Sydney.

But all around the world, in all the languages and lands,
There was one chant that all came to speak and understand.
And it could be heard clearly above the street clatter and chatter:
Black Lives Matter!

NEW GREEN BOOK, PAGE 1: TRAVELING WHILE BLACK

No implicit bias training necessary, I'm not going to fly,
book, board, or use points with American Airlines.
No need to drag me from your planes or kick me off your flights,
I understand perfectly that your kind of American means white.
Omg! You have the audacity to disrespect me with Black service fees!
No, before I fly with you, it'll be a long road trip for me.
Now that I've arrived at my destination, I need somewhere to stay.
There are so many options, so I must be smart about where I pay to lay.

Nope, not staying at the Hilton, Hampton, or the Arlo to be racially profiled.
After the humiliation goes viral, you want to reconcile.
Unh, unh, don't offer an empty apology, or tweet your corporate values
because your mistreatment of me is the truest reflection of you.
You walked past 100 white people in the lobby to ask the only Black
if I was a paying guest and wanted me to prove it at that.
Show you my room key and my ID,
and if I don't, you threaten to call the police?

I look like someone who shouldn't be here, can't be a guest?
You mean like that crazy white girl whom you didn't vet?
You know the one who assaulted a kid and all you did
was take her side, denigrate, humiliate, and continually insist
that your real guests comply with her outrageous request!
Well, now you have at least one patron less than yesterday.
Don't want to talk honey, just refund my money
because I did not enjoy my stay.

NEW GREEN BOOK, PAGE 2: SHOPPING WHILE BLACK

Publix, you need to understand that "I can't breathe"
is why Black Lives Matter is printed on your employees' masks and sleeves
and that the movement isn't political, it's about racial equality.
By the way, I'm not shopping for racism, I'm shopping for food
but you're in partnership with a donor of white supremacist groups.
Although you say the heiress of insurrection isn't associated with you,
She was president in '19, and you still cut her 20% checks. True?

While I'm out boycotting, I'll make a stop at Walmart
because it needs to be held accountable for playing an integral part
in funding politicians who incite racial division
and supporting for-profit companies that benefit
from keeping Blacks imprisoned.
Oh, about your bad corporate practices, why must a clerk unlock the case
so that I can purchase products for my black hair and face,
the door checker scrutinize my receipt because of my color,
and the cashier verify my ID and green but no other customer's?

Whew! Boycotting works up an appetite; it's time to eat.
Where can I find a Black-friendly establishment in these streets?
I asked for pepperoni on my pizza, not prejudice, Papa John's,
but you added Neo-Nazi, and I ordered extra Napoli and parmesan.
When I told the store clerk, Kevin, he caught an attitude,
and then I filed a complaint with Karen, the
manager, but she was extremely rude.

Not your concern, Mr. Founder? Wait, didn't you call me a racial slur, too?
Oh, you cleared yourself with your own investigation and
informed me, that "it wasn't directed at you."
and cited your past relationships with "prominent African Americans" as proof,

then claimed that your board used the black
community to steal your company from you.
Although you feel betrayed by the people you paid,
called it a "set up," and it may be so,
but we wouldn't know how you truly felt if you
weren't flipping your lips like pizza dough.

You, didn't learn from Cracker Barrel's, IHOP's,
and Denny's mistreatment of my hue?
Waffle House, bias and bigotry scattered, smothered,
chunked, and covered is difficult to chew.
Nope, that dish isn't on the menu, and it's not what
I ordered, but you delivered it anyway.
Now, I want my money back and free triple stack
because I don't appreciate the taste.

Starbucks, I could not pass by without addressing you, too
because you like to French press a flavor of bigotry with your brew.
Before I indulge on a cup of coffee or tea, do you mind if I pee,
or will my refusal to pay first warrant a visit from the local police?

There are too many restaurants to recite in this verse what I've learned.
Instead, I will leave this here for you because it should raise all our concern:

Restaurants have a new way to discriminate
against class and race during our time,
"No Ghetto Gear" and "No Tennis Shoes Here"
are the new "No Colored" signs.

DAT OLE FAMILIAR TUNE

We on da flo' dancin' to dat ole familiar tune,
♫ You equal to me, and I'm equal to you, ♫
But we all know that the song doesn't rang true
when Black *lives* hold less value than the *color* blue.

Still, we dance and dance and twirl each other 'round.
Wheeee! Wheeee! Oops, somebody's going down!
It is never you; naw, it's always undeservedly me
who fails ta' see that I cain't ever dance unreservedly.

But every time you invite me to da' flo',
I giddily accept like I don't know what I'm askin' fo',
and I dance and dance 'til I fall again,
or 'til dat ole familiar tune comes to an end.

TWO QUINTAINS FOR QUEENS WHO SANG

for all the beautiful, Black songstresses who soulfully sing/sang our stories

Beautiful Black Queens, sang, sang, sang!
Recording our hurt, narrating our pain –
Ballads and lyrics conveying our stories,
lamenting our losses, crooning our glories.
Sang, Black Queens, sang!

Beautiful Black Queens, sing, sing, sing!
Humming our hopes, serenading our dreams –
Moving melodies weaving our history in between
the seams of our souls, tattered, now whole, bellowing tales untold.
Sing, Black Queens, sing!

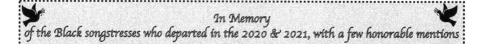

In Memory
of the Black songstresses who departed in the 2020 & 2021, with a few honorable mentions

Lena Horne
*Pamela Hutchinson
Josephine Baker   Phyllis Hyman   Nina Simone
Pearl Bailey   Mahalia Jackson   Bessie Smith
Dorothy Dandridge   Eartha Kitt   Donna Summer
Natalie Cole   Lisa Left-Eye Lopez   Sarah Vaughan
Aretha Franklin   *Duranice Pace   Dinah Washington
Billie Holiday   Della Reese   *Mary Wilson
Aaliyah Houghton   Nancy Wilson
Whitney Houston   *Betty Wright

They are listed in alphabetical order by last name. 2020 and 2021 deaths denoted by *. Please forgive any omissions. Charge it to my head, not my heart.

MY GRANDPARENTS' LIVING ROOM

*for the Black male musicians who make/made the musical memoirs of our lives
and for our grandfathers and grandmothers whose living rooms capture our stories*

Our ears dance and souls rejoice listening to the songs of our stories,
those *here and now*, that you recite in your oral and poetic histories,
narrating the pains, joys, losses, struggles, and victories of our time,
your voices move easily, gently *cruisin* on the notes and lyrics of our lives.

Your music is the soundtrack of all our family's many gatherings.
We're having one now; the entire family is here dancing and laughing.
Every year, every Christmas, it's pretty much the same,
we gather around the living room in my Grandparents' name.
All eyes are wide, and ears pricked because Grandfather is singing.
He doesn't sing much, but when he does, we listen intently
because there is a deep connection between his voice and heart,
and we're always stuck somewhere in the groove of its parts,
swaying gently to its rich and soulful timbre, captivated from the start.

This evening, Grandfather is singing about the ole days,
the agony and ecstasy of his boyhood years and of being
the *great-great grandson of a slave.*
His riffs and runs are very emotive, bellowing out sounds
about his life in that *Mississippi cotton pickin delta town* –
A time, when Black *fathers and sons* worked side by side
through *daylight and darkness,* backs bent, and feet tired.
Pickin and prickin, pickin and prickin, their fingers would bleed,
and then they'd drag themselves home to wash up, eat, and sleep,
singing *freedom blues* all the way there and back, then repeat.

D.B. MAYS

His eyes drift too long down that road of reminiscence;
thus, his solemn disposition has darkened the room a bit.
But Grandmother reaches out to touch his hand, rubbing it
and guiding him out the forest of long-ago before he gets lost in it.
She doesn't like him to go too far or to visit for too long
because, sometimes when he wanders, it's hard for him to return.
Still, she understands better than any of us what he's feeling now
and how difficult it is to balance the sow and the plow.
That's why she reminds him that "*those days are gone*, yes?
So, it's best not to dwell on the things *Miss Otis regrets*."

Gently released from his reverie, Grandfather nods his head,
offering her and us a reassuring smile as he brings his song to an end.
Surveying their living room, bigger than his boyhood's one-room building,
he offers a silent prayer of appreciation to God for *all his children*,
for living to see his legacy, and for having, as he sings from time to time,
"more than a *little joy* than I deserved at all in my lifetime."

He brings Grandmother's left hand to his lips, kisses it, tenderly tugs her ear.
She shoos him away, smiling bashfully, playing coy after all these years.

"You're *so amazing*," he serenades, nothing but warmth and love in his eyes.
"This *house is not a home* without you in it. I know I say it all the time.
Come on and *rip it up* with me on the dance floor this Christmas night."

She giggles like a schoolgirl, happily accepting his invite,
joining him on the floor, swinging her shapely hips from side to side,
and humming the melody of "Isn't She Lovely," one of their favorite tunes.
Smiles all around from young and old, we all clap and cheer them on,
singing along, happy that we get to see them as they are with us now,
while catching a glimpse of their love in bloom in
that *Mississippi cotton pickin delta town*.

When "My Girl" comes on, Grandfather invites
me to join their little adventure.
"Come dance with us, *Ebony eyes*," he calls, and the three of us dance together.

I'm their favorite grandchild, and I know it and show it; my name is Ebony.
I put on a grand display of it before all my cousins who snicker at me in envy.
My mother, my grandparents' eldest daughter, she pretends to be jealous, too.
She cuts in, whistling to me, "I'd like to *dance with my father*, now, scoot."

Pretending to be wounded, I release my Grandfather's hands,
but I'm still dancing on the inside, happy to see my mother be a little girl again.
Then my father takes Grandmother's hand, smiling with delight,
as he patiently waits his turn to take a dance with his own wife.
Father is ready to switch partners when a "Ribbon in the Sky" comes on,
and so, he asks my mother to slow dance to their wedding song.

"*My Cherie Amour*, may I take you around the bend a bit?"
She laughs at what he's told her, teasingly she rejects
him, and tells him to ask her again.
Grandfather smiles, and offers Father my mother's
hand, putting one into the other,
giving away the bride once more and slapping
Father affectionately on the shoulder.
Then he eagerly returns to his original dance partner,
a better version of his daughter, but older.

Pressing his cheek against Grandmother's, Grandfather bursts into song,
"*You've really got a hold on me*, woman. We can do this all night long."
She blushes, mouths a delicate whisper, barely
aloud, "Um, *I second that emotion*."
I shouldn't be eavesdropping on their intimate moment,
but I'm mesmerized by their devotion.

D.B. MAYS

Soaking it all in, I remember basking in the glow
of my grandparents' *endless love*.
Now that I am much older, I find myself reflecting on the journey of their love.
From the outside looking in, the life my grandparents
built is the American dream,
complete with a white house, picket fence, and children
to spare, the perfect American team.
But their story is not the quintessential American story some would sell it to be.
My grandparents realized and lived the *impossible
dream* – our ancestors' wildest dream.
The dream where a sharecropper with a 3rd grade
education and a life-long domestic are FREE
to be whomever and whatever they wanted to be,
carving out and shaping their own destiny.
FREE to *buy* and *own* a home, FREE to *have, keep,*
and *be with their children* all their lives,
and FREE to *choose* whomever they want to marry, to love, and be loved by.
I know, I digress, that's not the song we were listening
to – let me change the track back
so that we can enjoy the tunes, once more, that are
playing in my grandparents' living room.

"Junior, where's that woman, *Lucille*, who you brought around here last?"
Uncle Senior jests to his younger brother, smacking
his knee and taking the liberty to laugh.
"Yeah, Junior, she had a *whole lotta shaking goin on*. Where's she at now?"

Uncle Junior rolls his eyes, exasperated, his face scrunched in an irritated scowl.
"I ain't *going in circles* with that woman, I ain't seeing her no mo.
She can *keep a knockin* at somebody else's doe that's for sho!"

"What's that now," Grandfather quips, *"Ebony and Ivory* ain't gonna make it?"
Referencing how Uncle Junior was always making
up with some woman to break it.

Everybody is laughing at and with Uncle Junior by now, even us kids,
although we really aren't supposed to be listening in, but we did.
So, we continue pretending that we aren't here, but we're really in it;
we're always in it, listening, whispering, and slyly grinning.

Grandmother belts out, "Boy, when are you gonna *stop to love?*
You got to learn to *love the one you're with, stop chasin fires,*
just can't keep switching out women like you change out tires.
A relationship is just like life, there's *the agony and the ecstasy,*
and you can't have one without the other, mama's sweet baby."

She turns to Auntie who's been exceptionally quiet during this reception,
undoubtedly because she was hoping to escape Grandmother's attention.
"And this goes for you, too, missy. Good golly, Miss Molly!
Stop wasting time on a *part-time lover* when you
should be cuttin a tree, not pickin holly.
You need to look for a full-time love that doesn't come with strings attached.
The best things in life are free, girl. Keep chasin
money, watch out for what you attract."

Auntie, as my Grandmother likes to sing, is too busy *living for the city* to marry.
"Oh, mama, *don't you know that* everybody can't
have what you have with Daddy?"

Grandmother dismisses Auntie's customary retort,
singing another of her favorite tunes,
"Chile, please. You have to *wait for love.* Love
doesn't happen when we want it to.
Sometimes *it's gonna take a little bit longer* for love's *sunflowers* to bloom."

"Okay, you two," Grandfather intercedes; he knows
there will be *blood on the fields* soon;
it won't be Grandmother's blood either, it'll be
Auntie's on the floor of their living room.

D.B. MAYS

Forever her daddy's baby girl, Auntie, kisses Grandfather's cheek in gratitude.
He embraces her face with his hands, and gently brings her forehead to his lips,
kisses it softly, and offers her a pair of compassionate eyes before he begins with,
"Baby girl, *all I have to offer you* is this ...."

Smoothly, he backs up Grandmother, the way
he does, lifts up his voice, and sings,
"For you to love, the way your mother and I do, you have to be willing,
willing to give love in the same way that you want someone to give it to you.
Not halfway in and halfway out. Listen, I know you *don't want to be a fool,*
a fool for nobody, but you can't avoid crying the
tears of a clown from time to time.
Everybody has to be a fool at least once; I was once
your mother's fool, and she, too, was mine.
If you open your heart to the right clown, like we
did with each other, you will be all right."

Grandfather tenderly wipes the tears from her cheeks
and smiles, he doesn't want his baby blue.
Auntie dries her eyes, forces a laugh, and sighs, "Alright, daddy. I hear you."

Grandfather is gone now, and no one and nothing has been the same.
I assure you, the loss that we are feeling as a family is no *ordinary pain.*
Since Grandfather left, Grandmother wears a sadness on her face
that lets me and everyone else know that *love's in need of love today.*

At Grandfather's homegoing, Auntie climbs on top of his casket,
screaming, *"Give me the reason*, Lord! *Oh why!*" Horrified by her dramatics,
Uncle Junior warns, "You keep this up, they're
gonna put you in a straight-jacket."
Uncle Junior tries with all his might to pull his little sister her away,
but he struggles to keep her from jumping into their father's grave.
Lucille is back, and she tries to help Uncle Junior get Auntie to behave,
but Auntie thrashes about wildly, knocking Lucille to the ground
and, inadvertently, hitting Uncle Junior in the
mouth, nearly knocking his teeth out.

Rubbing his lips, Uncle Junior sits down, waving his hand in retreat.
Thinking of Grandfather, I suppress my laughter and smile, humming softly,
"Grandfather, I guess they're going to make it after all, *Ebony and Ivory.*"

The pallbearers take over, while Uncle Junior leans his head on Lucille,
who offers him a sympathetic *shoulder to cry on*, tissue, and an open ear.
Sitting to Grandmother's left, Uncle Senior bites
his bottom lip, crosses his arms.
Grandmother murmurs and sucks her teeth about how Auntie is carrying on.
Mother presses Grandmother's hand in agreement,
shaking her head in in dismay.
Wrapping an arm around Mother, Father suppresses
a chuckle about the events of the day.
At the repast, all us kids gather around and laugh
until our stomachs hurt on all sides.
Recapping Auntie's absurdity is the comedic relief
we need to help keep us from crying.
Grandfather's passing meant everything would change,
including our Christmases each year.
Thinking of his absence, I cry so much that my face
is streaked with *the tracks of my tears.*

I am okay until I venture into the kitchen for a
piece of pineapple upside down cake,
and see Mother's face buried in Father's chest; she's
sobbing, it's more than I could take.
"I wish I could *dance with my father* once more," I hear her moan, and I groan.
I quietly leave the entryway and retreat to the grandkids' bedroom, alone.
I cry until the well is dry, wiping the *tears on my pillow* and saying with a sigh,
"Grandfather, we're all *really gonna miss you.* I will remember you all my life."

It's hard as the weeks go by, *but I try*, to live the way Grandfather had in life
Most importantly, I spend a lot of time trying to
return joy to Grandmother's eyes.

D.B. MAYS

Concerned for Grandmother's melancholy, Mother
tries to provide her some relief.
"*If this world were mine*, Mama, I'd bring him back.
I'm can't, but *you can depend on me.*"

Grandmother offers Mother a sad smile before responding, in song,
"*After you put back the pieces, I'll still have a broken* heart, and I'll be alone.
Since I lost my baby, this *house is not a home*. Oh, *I'd rather* be ..."
She doesn't finish her statement, but we all know
where she was going with things.
Grandmother's heart is broken, eyes are vacant, the color is gone from her face.
Nothing and no one could *make it better*; shortly
after, she departed from this place.

Afraid, I remember pleading with her to stay, on her deathbed where she lay.
"Grandmother," I implored, "please *don't take away your love*. Don't go away.
Can Heaven wait for you, *if only for one night?* I can't lose you, too."

Grandmother offered me the best smile she could
and then clasped her hands in mine as she often would.
"*Ebony eyes*, you are *my girl, you are the sunshine of my life*,
but my *soul is responding* to and reaching for that *ribbon in the sky*.
Baby, Grandmother is already *halfway to paradise*, so let me fly.
Your grandfather is waitin to have *another dance* with me; time to let me go.
Being with you here on earth has been my great life's joy, but *Heaven knows
I'm leaving*, gonna *walk the proud land*, and when I get to that paradise above,
I'm gonna to *kiss an angel good morning*, and I'll be sure give him your love.
I know you're sad, but you'll understand someday
when you have a *love fire* like mine
that two things you can't take for granted in this life is love, darlin, and time."

Oh, this was *the day the world stood still*, and I felt my heart would break.
Where do I put her memory? I thought, as the Angel
of Death took Grandmother away.

Grandmother, you were right, I found my *always and forever.*
The love between me and my kids and my husband has been a great endeavor.
It is *a very special love* like the love you and Grandfather had together.

These are my thoughts as I roam the rooms of my grandparents' home.
Though they are both long gone from here, the *power of love* remains so strong.
Suddenly, I am much consumed by the energy I feel in their living room.
It's as if they are standing next to me; oh, how I so want to feel them near.
So, I ring their number from time to time, let
the message play so that I can hear,
"God bless you, friend. You've reached the loving home of Ebony and Duke,"
I smile, and through joyful tears, I sing to them, *"I just called to say I love you."*

In Memory
of the Black male musicians who departed in 2020 & early 2021, with one honorable mention

Roy Hammond,
Ellis Marsalis, Jr.,
Johnny Nash
Charley Pride
Little Richard
Luther Vandross
Bunny Wailer

Because you deserve your flowers now and your songs
have conveyed the Black experience for and through countless movements:

Smokey Robinson and Stevie Wonder

They are listed in alphabetical order by last name. Please forgive any omissions. Charge it to my head, not my heart.

BLACK HAVEN

When drops of hail plunge from the sky
wisps of wind sway far and high,
and tides come lunging in from sea,
You are the haven that shelters me.

When those cherished and dear deceive,
life's challenges are too much for me,
and the Devil attempts to seize my soul,
You are the haven that keeps me whole.

When the trials I face test my faith,
my voice falters, and my confidence breaks,
and I must search deep to find the courage within,
You are the haven that gives me strength.

When there's a light that I cannot see
because the darkness encompasses me,
and my heart aches evermore,
You are the haven I am searching for.

You are the sun in my life beaming brilliantly,
the light of my soul shining infinitely,
the peace in my heart easing life's pain,
You are my haven from the rain.

SOMEBODY
HAD TO DO IT

*for the Freedom Riders and Freedom Fighters whom we lost in
2020 and 2021: Congressman John Lewis, Reverend C.T. Vivian,
Rev. Dr. Joseph Lowery, Bruce Boynton, Mayor David Dinkins,
Texas State Rep Al Edwards, Rev. Darius L. Swan, Meredith C. Anding, Jr.*

Somebody had to do it
Integrate the South
Somebody had to do it
Walk that bridge for miles
Somebody had to do it
Boycott the bus
Somebody had to do it
Take Bloody Sunday beatings for us
Somebody had to do it
Freedom Ride Jim Crow
Somebody had to do it
So, they couldn't keep telling us, "No!"
Somebody had to do it
Challenge the right to vote at that courthouse
Somebody had to do it
Take that punch in the mouth
Somebody had to do it
Integrate the schools
Somebody had to do it
Read-ins at public libraries, too
Somebody had to do it
Sometimes crime does pay
Somebody had to do it
Legalize Juneteenth, celebrate Jubilee Day
Somebody had to do it

D.B. MAYS

Mobilize "The Harlem Gang of Four"
Somebody had to do it
Somebody had to say, "No more!"
Somebody had to do it
Commit American crimes
Somebody had to do it
To change the laws of our time
Somebody had to do it
Someone had to take the first step
Somebody had to do it
Even if that step ended in arrest or death.

A SEASON OF PROTEST:
WE WON'T STICK TO SPORTS

for the Hall of Famers of Sports Activism

"I am not going to stand up to show pride in a flag for a country that oppresses black people and people of color. To me, this is bigger than football and it would be selfish on my part to look the other way. There are bodies in the street and people getting paid leave and getting away with murder."
— *Colin Kaepernick, 2016, NFL Network Interview*

@Colin Kaepernick @NFL
Boy, you better *shut up*, and run that ball down the field.
We pay you a lot of money to make touchdowns,
not for you to kneel in protest against police brutality,
not for you to kneel during the national anthem to raise awareness about
"racial discrimination in this nation,"
and definitely not for you to kneel in protest of America's crimes against
Black humanity in the 21ˢᵗ Century.

@Elizabeth Williams @WNBA Atlanta Dream, @Lebron James @NBA
Girl, boy, you better *shut up*, and dribble those balls down the court.
We pay you a lot a money to make jump shots,
not for you to wear hoodies in protest against racial inequality and injustice,
not for you to lock arms to raise awareness for
racial violence against Black women,
and definitely not for you to take "collective actions"
against the American *flag*ging of Black citizens.

@Serena Williams, @Venus Williams, @Naomi Osaka @USTA
Girl, you better *shut up*, and swing that racket on the court in SILENCE.
We pay you a lot of money to make quiet shots,
not for you to have sit-outs in protest against Black oppression,

---

D.B. MAYS

not for you to wear masks to raise awareness for
Black victims of police violence,
and definitely not for you to "start a conversation"
about the U.S. genocide of Black
people "in a majority white sport."

@Bubba Wallace @NASCAR
Boy, you better *shut up*, and drive that car around the track.
We pay you a lot of money to make those laps,
not for you to protest the confederate flag as a symbol of racial oppression
or to demand its removal,
not for you to race your Black Lives Matter car
to raise awareness for discrimination,
and definitely not for you to be an "advocate for
Black Lives" and say that they "Matter"
in a predominantly white sport.

Girl, boy, you knew the expectations when you signed this deal.
Toe the line, or we'll take you from foot to heel,
We, the *real* American people feel,
that you should *shut up* and *stick to sports.*

Please delete those tweets because we, the Black American family,
understand and appreciate you for being champions of this fight.
We celebrate you for doing what's right and elevating our plight.
Together, we are proud to be Black, Black and proud, and we are proud
that you are using your sport to say and show our Blackness out loud.

So, play in protest, play to win, play until Black oppression ends.
Play until America's unjust systems break, not bend – *play until the end.*

Even Jackie Robinson, one of the greatest baseball players to ever play the game,
wouldn't sing the anthem or salute the flag,
but they filled the stadium all the same.

Still, the wheels of progress and justice are slow
as illuminated in the examples below.
We'll begin in '62 with Walter Beach, the AFL cut him for protesting Jim Crow.
In '67, they stripped Muhammad Ali of the title,
and exiled him from the boxing ring
because he stood in protest of the Vietnam War.
Now, was he right or was he wrong?
Depends on which side of history you were on, now
that the good 'ole days are long gone.

While America eventually respected his fight, at the
time, they said, *shut up*, and *toe the line*!
Met with vitriol and hate, Muhammad Ali is now
considered the greatest athlete to date.
He stood alone in his ring, but he sought comradery
with Black athletes across sports and teams.
Jim Brown, Bill Russell, Kareem Abdul Jabar and more
supported Ali, standing with him in solidarity
when it was an unpopular thing to do, but they were
more than players on the field and court.
Committed to elevating the Black plight and Civil
Rights, they said, "we won't *stick to sports.*"

Ali would not be the only athlete to sacrifice his career and his love of the sport.
The '68 Olympic sprinters and medalists were sports activist GOATS of sorts.
John Carlos and Tommie Smith used the Olympic
stage to highlight Black issues of the day.
Pumping Black Power fists in protest of racism, and much to America's dismay,
they did not sing the anthem or salute the flag
because they refused to *shut up and race.*

We understand and appreciate them for being champions of the fight.
We celebrate them for doing what's right and elevating our plight.
Together, we are proud to be Black, Black and proud, and we are proud
that they used their sport to say and show our Blackness out loud.

So, walk off the field
Run off the court
If you're not there,
nobody's watching that sport.
Don't stick to sports!

*Why do some Black people and Black athletes refuse
to sing the anthem or salute the flag?*
The lyrics of the national anthem stoke racial
violence and prejudice against Blacks.
Many Americans only know and sing the beginning
verses of the national anthem,
but it is with the third verse of "The Star-Spangled
Banner" that many Blacks take exception.
Its composer, Francis Scott Key, was a man who
advocated for and profited from slavery.
The Colonel Marines, under the British army,
defeated Key at the Battle of Bladensburg.
So perturbed by the battalion of hired runaway
"slaves," Francis Scott Key wrote this verse:

And where is that band *who so vauntingly swore, That
the havoc of war and the battle's confusion
A home and a Country should leave us no more?*
Their blood has wash'd out their foul footstep's pollution.
No refuge could save the hireling and slave
From the terror of flight or the gloom of the grave,
*And the star-spangled banner in triumph doth wave
O'er the land of the free and the home of the brave.
- "The Star-Spangled Banner," Verse 3*

To paraphrase, so that it is plain, Key writes that our
Black ancestors, the "hireling" and "slave,"
would be chased away or into their "grave" and, if
slain, "their blood" used to wash away
the "pollution" of the "foul" British army, who had
the audacity to let the enslaved be free
and defend their liberty; for wanting freedom, the
"hireling and slave" would receive no mercy.
America's anthem encourages our Black death and oppression
in perpetuity, as written by Francis Scott Key.

"The Star-Spangled Banner is as much a patriotic song as it is a diss track to black people who had the audacity to fight for their freedom." Jason Johnson, July 2016, The Root

HIGHLIGHTING ATHLETES AND THEIR ACTIVISM

Below are some of the most poignant statements and actions made over the years by Black athletes who have demonstrated solidarity in sports against Black oppression, racial violence, racial discrimination, inequality, and police brutality.

"I know that I am a black man in a white world. ... I cannot stand and sing the anthem. I cannot salute the flag; I know that I am a black man in a white world. In 1972, in 1947, at my birth in 1919, I know that I never had it made." Jackie Robinson, 1972, *I Never Had It Made*

"It was very important that you let people understand that you're more than a football player. Football is what I did, it wasn't who I was. Muhammad Ali was a boxer. That's what he did. That wasn't who he was, calling out injustice and insisting that human lives are more important than sport." – Walter Beach, 1967, on the Cleveland Summit/Muhammad Ali's Draft-Dodging Charges

"Why should they ask me to put on a uniform and go 10,000 miles from home and drop bombs and bullets on Brown people in Vietnam while so-called Negro people in

Louisville are treated like dogs and denied simple human rights? No, I'm not going 10,000 miles from home to help murder and burn another poor nation simply to continue the domination of white slave masters of the darker people the world over. This is the day when such evils must come to an end. ... The real enemy of my people is here. ... I have nothing to lose by standing up for my beliefs. So, I'll go to jail, so what? We've been in jail for 400 years." – Muhammad Ali, 1967, Public statement

"My interests have expanded in various areas—in racial relations, my various investments and, of course, my new movie career, but most of all in my sense of responsibility to my people. For the rest of my life, I am committed to taking part in the black struggle that's going on in this country" – Jim Brown, 1968, Alex Haley Interview

"The moral universe doesn't bend toward justice unless pressure is applied. In my seventh decade of hope, I am once again optimistic that we may be able to collectively apply that pressure, not just to fulfill the revolutionary promises of the U.S. Constitution, but because we want to live and thrive." – Kareem Abdul-Jabbar, July 2020, *LA Times*

"We have got to make the white population uncomfortable and keep it uncomfortable, because that is the only way to get their attention." – Bill Russell, 2018, *The Last Pass: Cousy, Russell, the Celtics, and What Matters in the End*

"There's a lot of racism in this country disguised as patriotism, and people want to take everything back to the flag, but that's not what we're talking about. We're talking about racial discrimination, inequalities and injustices that happen across this nation." – Colin Kaepernick, September 2016, *The Guardian*

@Carmelo Anthony, @LeBron James, @Chris Paul, and @Dwyane Wade, 2016 ESPYs

"The system is broken, the problems are not new, the violence is not new, and the racial divide definitely is not new, but the urgency for change is definitely at an all-time high" – Carmelo Anthony

"Tonight, we're honoring Muhammad Ali, the GOAT. But to do his legacy any justice, let's use this moment as a call to action to all professional athletes to educate ourselves, explore these issues, speak up, use our influence and renounce all violence and, most importantly, go back to our communities, invest our time, our resources, help rebuild them, help strengthen them, help change them. We all have to do better."
– LeBron James

"We stand before you as fathers, sons, husbands, brothers, uncles, and in my case, as an African-American man and the nephew of a police officer, who is one of the hundreds of thousands of great officers serving this country. But Trayvon Martin, Michael Brown, Tamir Rice, Eric Garner, Laquan McDonald, Alton Sterling, Philando Castile — this is also our reality." - Chris Paul

"The racial profiling has to stop. The shoot-to-kill mentality has to stop. Not seeing the value of black and brown bodies has to stop." – DeWayne Wade

"I wouldn't want to be any other color. There's no other race, to me, that has such a tough history for hundreds and hundreds of years, and only the strong survive, so we were the strongest and the most mentally tough, and I'm really proud to wear this color every single day of my life." – Serena Williams, December 2016, Common Interview, The Undefeated

"I've said this before. I've been said this for like the last couple months. Of course, I feel like he's being blackballed, obviously because of his position. … For Kaepernick to take that knee, it changed a lot of people's minds. It ruffled a lot of people's feathers. It ruffled a lot of locker rooms." – Michael Bennett, April 2017, The Undefeated

"Players have a responsibility to come together and respond collectively. There is now no doubt in my mind that what he [Kaepernick] did last season was a courageous, prophetic, self-sacrificial act that has captivated a nation and inspired a powerful movement." – Russell Okung, October 2017, The Players Tribune

"I'm a Pro Football Player Now, but I'll Be Black Forever" – Michael Bennett's, 2018, Things That Make White People Uncomfortable

---

@Serena Williams in response to Billie Jean King,
July 2019, Sports Center/Twitter
"The day I stop fighting for equality... will be the day I'm in my grave."

"This is about the biggest problems facing the game I love — and how we can fix them. I'm talking about the racism, misogyny, bullying and homophobia that permeates the culture of hockey. These issues have ramifications that most cannot — or will not — see. They are not fun to talk about. ... For every vocal racist, there's a thousand silent ones. ... What we CAN do is be courageous. ... What we CAN do is stand up for one another. ... Hockey is not for everyone. Not yet. But it damn sure should be." – Akim "Dreamer" Aliu, May 2020, *The Players Tribune*

@Venus Williams, June 2020, Instagram
"Speaking up about racism in the past was unpopular. It was shunned. No one believed you. Just as sexism is not only a 'women's issue'; racism is not only a 'black issue."

@Bubba Wallace, June 2020, Twitter:
"My next step would be to get rid of all Confederate flags. No one should feel uncomfortable when they come to a NASCAR race. So, it starts with Confederate flags. Get them out of here. They have no place for them."

@Richard Sherman about @Bubba Wallace's protest, June 2020, Twitter:
"I respect it. This is change. This fan base isn't the most diverse or inclusive and takes a lot of courage to take this stand in this sport."

@Naomi Osaka, August 2020, Instagram:
"... before I am an athlete, I am a Black woman. ... I don't expect anything drastic to happen with me not playing, but if I can get a conversation going in a majority white sport, I consider that a step in the right direction. ...Watching the continued genocide of Black people at the hand of the police is honestly making me sick to my stomach ...."

@GeorgeHill, Milwaukee Bucks player,
August 2020, NBA/Bucks Press conference
"I don't think we should be talking about basketball today. We should talk about the Blake family and what's going on."

@AtlantaDream player, @ElizabethWilliams, August 2020, Twitter
"We stand in solidarity with our brothers in the NBA and will continue this conversation with our brothers and sisters across all leagues and look to take collective action."

THE BATON

for the Black elders of every family, organization, field, and industry

The young will save the world.
With tolerance and charity,
they will reimagine society.

It does not matter what we think.
Tomorrow belongs to the young –
It's not intended for you and me.

The young will save the earth.
With conservation and reduction,
they will renew and restore it from
our destruction.

It does not matter what we think.
Tomorrow belongs to the young –
It's not intended for you and me.

The young will rebuild the nation.
With novel ideas and fresh perspectives,
They will redefine democracy with new
electorates and laws that are corrective.

It does not matter what we think.
Tomorrow belongs to the young –
It's not intended for you and me.

Pass the baton and move along.
We've held the role for far too long,
We did it our way, right or wrong.

Guide and advise but let them be.
Tomorrow belongs to the young,
It's not intended for you and me.

Acknowledge when the circle of life has spun.
Our time to govern the earth is done,
So, leave it to the young.
Pass the baton.

THE INVITATION

Death comes for us all,
steadily and slowly but most assuredly.
She dances a waltz to our life's end
with a natural turn,
assisting our step forward, we bend
as our souls rise at the end.
Death gracefully leads us
into our ethereal essence,
glides us away from life's core,
or plays a calamitous tune of woe
until we are no more.

Death comes for us all,
how we leave this life depends on how we live it.
She beckons us with a soft and lingering kiss,
an invitation so appealing, we cannot resist.
Still, we meet her lips in reluctant reception;
She smiles knowingly as she ingests our souls with deep affection.
Death artfully lures us into her unrelenting embrace,
wraps us in obscurity or releases us to the light –
Either way, we will go mercilessly or gently into thy good night,
and surrender willingly or grudgingly to everlasting respite.

LEGACY

Of my life, to whom do I have to give?
What charities to show for the years that I have lived?

What edifice will be constructed in memory?
What day will be commemorated in reverence to me?

What evidence will there be of the things I have done,
the people I have met, and the places I have gone?

None.

ODE TO BLACK PANTHER

for Chadwick Boseman, the human, son, husband, brother, and man

Beauty personified, epitome of elegance,
Sleek coat of black silk shining through ebony undertones,
A vision of unmitigated Black excellence,
An indelible footprint cemented where're he roams.

High neck steady on broad shoulders,
Chiseled chin tilted slightly in prominence,
Muscles protruding from his chest like boulders,
Deep-set eyes, unblinking Black dominance.

Moving stealthily, like a ghost in the forest,
Thou art quiet and elusive, unseen and unheard.
'Press on with pride and with purpose' – aphorist,
Whispering wisdom with very few words.

O' mighty Black Panther, thou art not fallen,
Rise and scale the mount and ascend to the ethereal throne.
Immortal Black Panther, thou countenance solemn,
Pensively peering from thy perch, surveying the land thou roam.

Night stalker, protector of the universe, tactically poised to attack.
Black Panther, our fierce guardian – supremely and splendidly Black.

ELEGY TO BLACK PANTHER

for Chadwick Boseman, the actor, and all the fans
who loved him as the Black Avenger

Yibambe, Mfalme, yibambe on your crossing to the ancestral land[1]
where we imagine the Infinity Gauntlet sitting safely upon your taloned hand.
Rest in power, Mfalme, sleep peacefully, for your earthly battles are won; [2]
The King of Wakanda forever, our most esteemed, Native son.

Here lies the story of Chadwick, the real-life hero of our time.
His ascent to the throne was arduous; his reign cut short during his prime.

A mysterious mass threatened the trajectory of our beloved King,
the dark matter would ravage his body, consuming his entire being.
To destroy the alien invasion, the Reality Stone he would need.
To remain in orbit around the sun, he would need to defy gravity.

"Take the Power Stone," we pleaded. "You could exert its energy
To eradicate the malady, overcome any challenge, and defeat any enemy."
When told it would perfect his condition, he proclaimed, "I like ambiguity.
Life isn't perfectly good, and life isn't perfectly bad.
I tried living my purpose and to do the most with the life I had."

When granted an alternate future, where he'd be resistant to disease,
a reversal of time was tempting, tipping the scales of certainty.
But when offered the coveted Time Stone, the
most modest of monarchs declined,
"The clock is ticking," he responded and lived his life as if on borrowed time.

---

1   Yibambe: In isiXhosa, it is a war cry that means "hold off," "hold fast", or "hold strong."
2   Mfalme: In Swahili, it means "king."

D.B. MAYS

The people thought their King had fallen, perceiving him as frail and weak.
Though they were astounded by his deportment and mocked him mercilessly,
he refused to use the Mind Stone to garner any public empathy.
Instead, he trekked discreetly, for blessed are the meek.

Oh, if we could wield the Space Stone to create
a portal from whence, he'd appear!
Though Heaven has called home its angel, we'd
rather our treasured T'Challa was here.
Had he rallied us with the war cry. "Yibambe! On your left," he'd hear us sing.
The Wakandan portal would materialize the stately
silhouette and regal, reassuring nod of our King.

So that he could live forever, there are a few wanton souls for sure
That we'd sacrifice for the Soul Stone, so our beloved
King could orbit the sun once more.
'Til then, we will look after one another, as if we are one single tribe;
To our King, Wakanda forever, we'll mourn you until the end of time.

IN MEMORY OF
BLACK MAMBA

for Kobe Bryant, my son, and all the kids who loved the Black Mamba

Sub-Saharan, long, agile, and thin
Mamba Mentality – snakelike precision,
Incredible speed, run with the wind, strike!
Strike! Sudden movement, opponents paralyzed, venomous bite.

Defensive posture, piercing black eyes keen, tongue flicks,
Palm overturned, coffin-shaped head projecting from an arched wrist.
Venom released, hear the hiss of the ball soaring in the air,
the distance is significant, but the ball still makes it there.

Rarely miss the target, expert shooter at long range,
the Black Mamba is one of the greatest ever to play the game.

"Aggressive, ... combative, confrontational, and cutthroat,"
when predators block movements, Mamba is easily provoked.
Form lithe like a snake, shape streamlined like an S,
mouth opens in warning; fangs erect ready to inject.

Mamba's in the trap, seemingly, with nowhere to go,
deep in the corner, he starts shooting threes from the floor.
Basketball immortal, a master of the sport,
"Destroying everybody that is stepping on the court."

Natural predator, arms pulled back in attack, poised on the tip of the tail,
Threes were on fire in Portland, venom blazing the trail.
81 points, almost caught Wilt in '06 against the Raptors that night,
Forty-eight minutes of magic and a career highlight.

Envenomating competitors in a series of rapid strikes.
Thus, he has a countless number of career highlights:

Two Olympic gold medals, five NBA rings,
18-time All-Star; four All-Star and two finals MVPs.
'06 and '07, the Black Mamba led scoring in the league,
a career total of fifteen All-NBA Teams.

Twenty-six 50-point games, six times Black Mamba scored 60,
The last time Kobe did this, it was in '16 with a 101 victory.
One year later, the Lakers retired No. 24 and No. 8,
as there was no debate that Kobe will forever be a Lakers' Great.

Shoot with the best, drive if pressed,
game-winning shots find the open man with less.
Made LA history with O'Neal and Phil,
adopted the moniker, Black Mamba, after watching *Kill Bill*.

Critics say the Mamba was selfish; charity, a trait he lacked.
A ball hog since boyhood, the Black Mamba confirming it as fact.
Kobe may have been guilty of shooting too much since age 8,
but how else would the Black Mamba become an NBA great?

Dear Basketball,
Here lies the Black Mamba, one of the best ballers of all time,
a #girldad of four, husband, brother, and son cut short in his prime,
a basketball immortal, a GOAT of all sports,
may the numbers 8 and 24, together, rule the ethereal court.

IMITATION OF LIFE

for the Black actors and actresses living and departed

How would we know what family, love, laughter,
joy, pain, struggle, loss, and overcoming
look, feel, and sound like
if not for your expressions of life moving
across the screen helping us to see
how much more to life there is
and how much more in this life we could be?

Your art helps us to understand people
who think, look, speak, and believe
differently than we.
Enlightened by these insights
that we gain from your expressions
on the screen,
we become more tolerant,
empathetic, and appreciative
of the people we thought
we didn't want to know,
the places we thought
we didn't want to see,
the foods we thought
we didn't want to eat,
and the human beings
we didn't know we could be.

In Memory
of the Black actors and actresses who departed in 2020 and 2021

Cecily Tyson

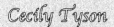

Raymond Allen
Chadwick Boseman
Thomas Jefferson Byrd
Natalie Desselle-Reid
Janet Dubois

Tony "Tiny" Lister
Marion Ramsey
Esther Scott
Carol Sutton
Dearon Thompson

They are listed in alphabetical order by last name. Please forgive any omissions. Charge them to my head, not my heart.

AMERICAN SOUP

We've taken the lid off,
the pot is boiling over.
Watch yourself, don't touch it
lest you burn and bear the scars
of that good ole American melting pot
that's cracking under the weight of its faux democracy.

My truthful review of your Good American soup?
I do not like the way it tastes, it's unsavory.
Because you separated each ingredient by group,
everything is all over the place –
onions here, tomatoes, potatoes, and carrots there,
and brown rice waaaayyy over there,
usually floating at the bottom of the pot
and hidden beneath everything else.
When you scoop a helping,
you only get the foam floating at the top
because no one took the time
to mixed the ingredients all together
or continually stir the soup as it simmered.
Anybody knows that for a Good American soup
to blend properly, you can't rush it,
you have to take your time and slow cook it
so that its unique flavors blend,
and the soup is cooked all the way through.

It isn't fragrant, appetizing, or appealing
either; you tossed everything into the pot
without giving it a second thought.
Anybody knows that for a Good American soup
to have a pleasant, savory aroma,
the ingredients need to be browned.

Your response to my review of your Good American soup?
You add a dash more of anything white –
salt, yogurt, or sour cream,
but it doesn't enhance the flavor.
It's simply bland.
Anybody knows that for a Good American soup
to be flavorful, richer,
you can't add salt without pepper.

RACISM

Rationalized false sense of physical, cultural, and intellectual superiority,

Antagonistic acts directed against my race and ethnicity,

Classification systems designed to protect your perceived white privilege,
oppress my Black and keep your knee to my neck and at the center of my back.

Ideologies of extremism to reinforce fictionalized
inferiority and promote white supremacy.

Systems and structures in place to perpetuate discrimination on the basis of race
restrict access and opportunity to advantage white
people and disadvantage Black people.

Marginalize melanated people based on a racial hierarchy that doesn't exist
because you are threatened of being the minority
and have a false sense of superiority.

2045 is coming, it's coming.

THE PREDATOR AND
THE PREY

The racial dynamics of America is one of the predator and the prey.
The prey is fixated on reaching compromise, maintaining harmony,
or camouflaging itself,
hoping to deceive the predator into believing the prey is something
other than what the predator already understands the prey to be.
The predator cannot be dissuaded because it breeds and feeds on hate
from one generation to the next, metamorphosing its appearance
and behaviors so that its malformations are unrecognizable to the prey.
To its own detriment, the prey is predictive in its movement,
and its response to the chase, capture, and kill, making it easy
for the predator to anticipate and attack and almost without challenge.

Driven by intense hunger, the predator does everything to corner, catch,
and consume anything that threatens its survival in the ecosystem.
To optimize its success for survival, it adapts, becoming a conventional
social predator that hunts, kills, and eats in its group of three: racism.
In its racist state, the predator is vulture-like, cluster hunting
and manipulating its members – bigotry, prejudice, and discrimination
to subdue and ruthlessly oppress its prey.
This tiered, tri-effort takes some planning to
enact, but it is a well-balanced system
of persecution that the predator has masterfully executed for centuries.

The dense and indolent, tertiary predator, bigotry, sits-and-waits for its prey,
ambushing the most vulnerable, usually, the young and defenseless prey.
The secondary predator, prejudice, is slightly more skilled and deceptive at
stalking its prey, using camouflage for cover and hiding behind uniforms
and societal and organizational roles, positioning itself to strike
and apprehend the prey at the most opportune and unsuspecting time.

The primary predator, discrimination, expertly
uses its social mechanisms to observe,
its institutions to predict, its legal system to
intercept, and its justice system to attack,
creating a sophisticated catchall system of suppression.

Racism is one of the most tyrannical and difficult perils
for the prey to escape because it does not evolve to protect itself.
If the prey struggles to adapt a good defense, the prey will
become extinct or complete fall. Either way, the predator
will move onto the next most vulnerable population,
scavenger hunting people of color until there are
none left but their own grandchildren.
Perhaps the nature of this interaction is parasitism not predation;
the predator is really a parasite feeding off its primary host for centuries,
unable to kill it because the parasite needs the host,
debilitated or otherwise, to survive.

BLACKNESS

The essence of ebony, the core of coal,
Black is the elegant and splendid hue of night.
Black is the fiery fever in the midst of cold,
The bearer of light and the giver of life.
Her fruitful womb from which all life blooms,
Black is the raven nurturing the Earth with flesh and bread
Black is the loam to which all life resumes,
Her heralder, keeper of souls, courier of the dead.
Why does Black not yield, break, or bend?
Black is the color of courage, an emblematic representation
Of dominance – yes, Black is power, Black transcends.
Black is prominence, a metaphysical manifestation
Of the Most High from which all men descend,
Black is the first, the beginning, the last, and the end.

HOW IT'S GOING DOWN

because sometimes we just need to vent about this shit to move on from it

You fucked with the last generation,
We're going to burn this bitch to the ground,
We're not casting any more votes
because this system is a joke!
The system isn't broken; it was built this way
to terrorize, oppress, and keep Black people enslaved.
It was never broken; it was built to exist like this.
And for this ... for it ... for all this shit,
your blood will spill into the streets,
and your rotten fruit will hang from trees
for the unspeakable things you did to me
my legacy, and my ancestry.

You fucked with the last generation,
We're going to burn this bitch to the ground!

EXISTING WHILE BLACK

To be Black in America is to live in a constant state of rage
Because anything we do or say can be used to justify our end,
Whatever that end may be – imprisonment, disenfranchisement, even death.

To be Black in America is to exist in a perpetual state of nonexistence
And live with Black restrictions and dire consequences
For simply existing and doing ordinary, everyday things.

To be Black in America, you must learn how to
move through the alphabet of life.
For culture vultures who want to live in the skin
we're in, look, talk, and walk like us,
You must place your hand on this book and repeat, "in Black we trust."

And then swear you'll learn and live by the ABC's
Of what it means to be Black like me.
To be Black in America means that it's harder or impossible for
you to do the following without being belittled, harassed, hated,
harmed, mocked, ostracized, scrutinized, and, sometimes, killed.

A
Achieve while Black –
Adopt children of another race while Black –
Advocate while Black –
Aid others while Black –
Answer questions while Black –
Apologize while Black –
Appoint while Black –
Arrested without harassment or harm while Black –
Arrest white people while Black –
Ask questions while Black –

Assert while Black –
Associate with questionable people while Black –
Audition while Black –

B
Backpack while Black –
Ballet while Black –
Bank while Black –
Barbeque while Black –
Baseball while Black –
Basketball while Black –
Be a child while Black –
Be a professional in any field while Black –
Be affluent while Black –
Be afraid while Black –
Be aggressive while Black –
Be ambitious while Black –
Be angry while Black –
Be an activist while Black –
Be an addict while Black –
Be an athlete while Black –
Be beautiful while Black –
Be blameless while Black –
Be in your home while Black –
Be intelligent while Black
Buy or sell a house while Black –
Be a grandma while Black –
Be a man while Black –
Be a parent while Black –
Be a tourist while Black –
Be a woman while Black –
Be a YouTuber while Black –
Bike while Black –
Brandish a gun while Black –
Breastfeed while Black –
Breathe while Black –

D.B. MAYS

Broadcast while Black –
Broker a deal while Black –
Budget while Black –
Buy anything while Black –

C
Carry anything in your pockets while Black –
Carry weapons while Black –
Cater while Black –
Celebrate while Black –
Challenge the system while Black –
Chaperone while Black –
Cheer while Black –
Command while Black –
Compete while Black –
Conceal weapons while Black –
Congregate while Black –
Contribute while Black –
Converse while Black –
Cook while Black –
Copulate while Black –
Counsel while Black –
Criticize while Black –
Cry while Black –
Curse while Black –

D
Dance while Black –
Date a non-Black person while Black –
Defend yourself or your family while Black –
Delegate while Black –
Deliver packages while Black –
Demand respect, justice, equality, and equity while Black –
Deny accusations while Black –
Detain anyone while Black –
Dine in a restaurant while Black –

Disagree with authorities while Black –
Disobey authorities or rules while Black –
Do anything illegal while Black –
Drink at a bar while Black –
Drive while Black –

E
Eat while Black –
Educate while Black –
Elect government officials and have your vote counted while Black –
E-mail while Black –
Emigrate while Black –
Enforce rules while Black –
Enfranchise while Black –
Engage in legal or illegal activities and live while Black –
Enlist in the military while Black –
Enter your own home while Black –
Entertain while Black –
Excel while Black –
Exercise while Black –
Exercise your civic duty while Black –
Exonerate while Black –
Express yourself while Black –

F
Fail while Black –
Fake anything while Black –
Fall while Black –
Farm while Black –
Father a child while Black –
Fatherhood while Black –
Ferry while Black –
Film the police while Black –
Finance while Black –
Find fault while Black –

D.B. MAYS

Finish first, better, or best while Black –
Fish while Black –
Flirt while Black –
Fly while Black –
Football while Black –
Forget while Black –
Franchise while Black –
Fraternize while Black –
Furlough while Black –

G

Garden while Black –
Gas up while Black –
Gender assign while Black –
Gentrify while Black –
Gerrymander while Black –
Get a fair chance while Black –
Get a promotion while Black –
Get a raise while Black –
Get a second chance while Black –
Get a warning ticket while Black –
Get help while Black –
Get justice while Black –
Get kidnapped while Black –
Get lost while Black –
Girl Scout while Black –
Golf while Black –
Go home while Black –
Go to predominantly white college while Black –
Go to a white friend's house while Black –
Govern while Black –
Graduate salutatorian or valedictorian while Black –
Graduate while Black –
Graffiti while Black –
Greet while Black –

Grieve while Black –
Give up while Black –
Grow up while Black –

H
Half-ass anything while Black –
Halloween while Black –
Handicap while Black –
Hangout while Black –
Happy hour while Black –
Hard-nose while Black –
Have babies while Black –
Have a misunderstanding while Black –
Have a party while Black –
Head Start while Black –
Help while Black –
Hike while Black –
Hit anyone or anything while Black –
Hope for better days while Black –
Hunt while Black –

I
Ideological while Black –
Idiotic while Black –
Indigenous while Black –
Idle while Black –
Indulgent while Black –
Inherit while Black –
Ignorant while Black –
Ignore while Black –
Illegal while Black –
Imagine while Black –
Imitate while Black –
Immigrate while Black –
Immoral while Black –
Impatient while Black –

Impeachable while Black –
Imperfect while Black –
Impersonal while Black –
Impolite while Black –
Impractical while Black –
Impulsive while Black –
Intern while Black –
Interview while Black –
Intimidate while Black –

J
Jail while Black –
Jaywalk while Black –
Jog while Black –
Join a predominately white institution or organization while Black –
Joke while Black –
Journey while Black –
Judge while Black –
Jump while Black –
Justify while Black –
Just live while Black –

K
Karate while Black –
Kayak while Black –
Kickstart while Black –
Kindergarten while Black –
Kneel for justice while Black –
Knock on a white person's door while Black –
Know too little while Black –
Know too much while Black –

L
Labor while Black –
Landlord while Black –
Landscape while Black –

Laugh while Black –
Lawyer up while Black –
Lead while Black –
Learn while Black –
Lease while Black –
Lecture while Black –
Lie while Black –
Lifeguard while Black –
Little League while Black –
Listen to music while Black –
Live in America while Black –
Live in a white community while Black –
Locksmith while Black –
Loiter while Black –
Look at a white person while Black –
Lose while Black –
Love while Black –

M

Make a mistake while Black –
Manage non-black people while Black –
Medicate while Black –
Middle class while Black –
Miss something while Black –
Misrepresent while Black –
Misunderstand while Black –
Mobilize while Black –
Model while Black –
Monopolize while Black –
Mother a child while Black –
Mourn while Black –
Move while Black –

N

Nap while Black –
Nationalize while Black –

Navigate while Black –
Need help while Black –
Need the police while Black –
Neglect while Black –
Negotiate while Black –
Neighbor while Black –
Nervous breakdown while Black –
Neutralize a threat while Black –
Nurse while Black –

O

Object while Black –
Observe while Black –
Occupy while Black –
Offend while Black –
Omit while Black –
Open house while Black –
Operate while Black –
Oppose while Black –
Order while Black –
Organize while Black –
Overcome while Black –
Own a business while Black –
Own a home while Black –

P

Parole while Black –
Panic while Black –
Perform while Black –
Pissed while Black –
Piss in public while Black –
Pitch while Black –
Playful while Black –
Play sports while Black –
Post on social media while Black –
Practice medicine while Black –

Pray while Black –
Pre-school while Black –
Proficient while Black –
Progress while Black –
Protest while Black –

Q

Qualify while Black –
Qualified while Black –
Quarantine while Black –
Quarrelsome while Black –
Quarterback while Black –
Queer while Black –
Question an officer while Black –
Question a white person while Black –
Quick-witted while Black –
Quiet while Black –
Quit while Black –

R

Race while Black –
Raise money while Black –
Reach too far or too high while Black –
React while Black –
Read while Black –
Real estate while Black –
Rebellious while Black –
Recant while Black –
Recycle while Black –
Referee while Black –
Rehabilitate while Black –
Relax while Black –
Remorseful while Black –
Rent while Black –
Research while Black –
Reside in your home while Black –

Rest while Black –
Retire while Black –
Rich while Black –
Rude while Black –
Run away while Black –
Run while Black –

S

Say, "No," while Black –
School while Black –
Scream while Black –
Seek help while Black –
Sell products on the street while Black –
Shoot while Black –
Shop while Black –
Sick leave while Black –
Sick pay while Black –
Sightsee while Black –
Sing while Black –
Single parent while Black –
Skateboard while Black –
Sleep while Black –
Snowboard while Black –
Socialize while Black –
Speak while Black –
Sportscast while Black –
Stay at a hotel while Black –
Study while Black –
Suburb while Black –
Succeed while Black –
Supervise non-black people while Black –
Support other Black people while Black –
Surrender while Black –
Sweepstakes while Black –
Swim in your own HOA pool while Black –

T

Talented while Black –

Talkative while Black –

Taxi while Black –

Teach non-black students while Black –

Teach black students while Black –

Theme park while Black –

Threatened or threaten while Black –

Tire while Black –

Transgender while Black –

Travel while Black –

Trust anyone while Black –

U

Be ...

Unaccountable while Black –

Unauthorized while Black –

Unaware while Black –

Uncertain while Black –

Uncensored while Black –

Unconscious while Black –

Unfit to serve while Black –

Uninhibited while Black –

Unionized while Black –

Unprofessional while Black –

Unsuccessful while Black –

V

Vacation while Black –

Vacation with white people while Black –

Vaccinate while Black –

Valiant while Black –

Valued while Black –

Victim or victimized while Black –

Victorious while Black –

Vigilant while Black –

Vindictive while Black –

Virtuous while Black –
Visible while Black –
Vociferous while Black –
Voluptuous while Black –
Vote while Black –
Vulnerable while Black –

W

Walk home while Black –
Walk pets while Black –
Weak while Black –
Wealthy while Black –
Weaponized while Black –
Wear a hoodie while Black –
Wear your natural hair while Black –
Weary while Black –
Well-dressed while Black –
Well-informed while Black –
Well-read while Black –
Well-spoken while Black –
Well-thought-of while Black –
Whisper while Black –
Woke while Black –
Work-study while Black –
Work while Black –
Wreck a vehicle while Black –

X

Be ...
Xany while Black –
Xenagogues while Black –
Xenas while Black –
Xenial while Black –
Xenodochial while Black –
Xenophobic while Black –

Y

Yawn while Black –
Yearn for more while Black –
Yell while Black –
Yield while Black –
Youthful while Black –
Young while Black –
YMCA while Black –

Z

Zany while Black –
Zappy while Black –
Zazzy while Black –
Zealful while Black –
Zen while Black –
Zoom with white colleagues while Black –

Most of all, to be Black in America means that you can't ...
Live freely, equally, and peacefully while Black
And die with dignity while Black.

D.B. MAYS

PART II

BLACK LIVES

*A Woeful, Poetic Account of Black Lives
Lost to Racial Violence & Police Brutality*

RIP - IN MEMORARIUM

Rest in Power, Rest in Protest, Rest in Peace

I am my brothers and sisters' keeper,
and for you, my brothers and sisters, I speak
through these lowly lines of poetry
to reverently record your collective release
from racial violence, injustice, and police brutality
and, most importantly, to elevate your memories.

I did not write a poem for every life lost, but I hope the poems I have included illuminate the individual and collective experiences of all who perished and honor the memories of those, listed and not listed here.

In Memory
of the Black lives lost to racial violence and police brutality from the late 20th to early 21st Centuries

Carlos Alcis
Clinton R. Allen
Raymond Allen, Jr.
Wendell Allen
Javier Ambler
Tanisha Anderson
Ahmaud Arbery
Alonzo Ashley
Aaron Bailey
Orlando Barlow
Jordan Baker
Ronald Beasley
Sean Bell
Vincent V. Belmonte
Anton LaRue Black
Jacob Blake
Sandra Bland
Rekia Boyd
Emantic "EJ" Bradford, Jr.
Rumain Brisbon
James Brissette
Rayshard Brooks
Michael Brown
Raheim Brown, Jr.
Eleanor Bumpurs
Aaron Campbell
Miriam Carey
Kiwane Carrington
Carlos Carson
Chavis Carter
Philando Castile
Terry J. Caver
Kenneth Chamberlain, Sr.
Quwan Charles
Alexia Christian
Jamal O'Neal Clark
Stephon Clark
McKenzie Cochran
John Crawford III
Charleston 9
Depayne M. Doctor
Cynthia Graham Hurd
Susie Jackson
Ethel Lee Lance
Clementa C. Pinckney
Tywanza Sanders
Daniel L. Simmons
Sharonda C. Singleton
Myra Thompson
***

Angelo "AJ" Crooms
Terrence Crutcher
Reynaldo Cuevas
Mcihelle Cusseaux
Dannette Daniels
Deborah Danner
Jordan Davis
Shantel Davis
Tyree Davis
Amadou Diallo
Keyarika Diggles
Nehemiah Dillard
Reginal Doucet
Samuel Dubose
Gregory Lloyd Edwards
Jordan Edwards
Sharmel Edwards
Manuel Elijah Ellis
DeAunta T. Farrow
Malcom Ferguson
Jonathan Ferrell
George Floyd
Janisha Fonville
Ezell Ford
Shereese Francis
Desmond Franklin
Shelly Marie Frey
Kanisha Necole Fuller
Korryn Gaines
Eric Garner
Bijan Ghaisar
Brendon Glenn
Clifford Glover
Henry Ace Glover
Pearlie Golden
Casey Goodson
Oscar Grant III
Freddie Gray
Kimani KiKi Gray
Ronald Greene
Jersey Green
Willie Howard Green
Akai Gurley
Latanya Haggerty
Dontre Hamilton
Darnisha D. Harris
Eric Harris
Danroy DJ Henry
Nicholas Heyward
Sterling Lapree Higgins

Andre Maurice Hill
Meagan Hockaday
Larry E. Jackson, Jr.
Kenya Sarie James
Botham Jean
Atatiana Jefferson
Ervin Lee Jefferson
Aleah Jenkins
Katherine Johnston
Aiyana Stanley Jones
Alberta Odell Jones
Bettie Jones
Corey Jones
Derrick Jones
Jonas Joseph
India Kager
Dijon Durand Kizzee
Kyam Livingston
Manual Loggins, Jr.
Andy Lopez
Charleena Chavon Lyles
Ronald Madison
Joseph Curtis Mann
Trayvon Martin
Tyisha Shenee Miller
Margaret Mitchell
David McAtee
Renisha McBride
Elijah McClain
Kendric McDade
Tony McDade
Jeremy McDole
Laquan McDonald
Della McDuffie
Tommy D. McGlothen, Jr.
Natasha McKenna
Nelson M. Mendez
Jamaal Moore, Sr.
Kayla Moore
Dr. Susan Moore
Patrick Moses
Earl Murray
John Elliot Neville
Gabriella Nevarez
Chinedu Okobi
Alfred Olango
Noel Palanco
Dante Parker
Frankie Ann Perkins
Sincere Pierce

Marlene Pinnock
Dennis Plowden
Dante Price
Jonathan D. Price
Sheneque Proctor
Daniel Prude
Angelo Quinto
Michael Brent Ramos
Dreasjon "Sean" Reed
Jerame Reid
Tamir Rice
Chad Robertson
Tamon Robinson
Tony Robinson
Antwan Rose, Jr.
Aura Rosser
Charles Roundtree, Jr.
Timothy Russell
Walter Scott
Priscilla Slater
Yvette Smith
Alberta Spruill
Timothy Stansbury, Jr.
Victor Steen
Alton Sterling
Terrence Sterling
Marcellis Stinnette
Breonna Taylor
Demarco Taylor
Sonji Taylor
Alesia Thomas
Timothy D. Thomas
Pamela Turner
Saheed Vassell
Sharon Walker
Johnnie K. Warren
Patrick L. Warren, Sr.
Steven Washington
Shulena Weldon
Barrington BJ Williams
Derek Williams
Malissa Williams
Tarik Wilson
Philip G. White
Victor White III
Tyree Woodson
Alteria Woods
Ousmane Zongo

The names are listed alphabetically. If there any omissions or misspellings, I apologize.
Charge it to my head and not my heart. Please see the "Bibliography" for the list of sources used.

HIGH BEAMS ON
A DARK, DUSKY ROAD

for Javier Ambler and other Black people "Distressed while Black"

The night had two settings, high and low
One light dimmed, while the other glowed
for a live life-sacrifice on a TV show
that captured on camera four electric shocks,
zooming in on the failure of his congestive heart.
Still, the cameramen's shooting did not stop
and neither did the cops.

Apparently, the contract with *Live PD*
impaired human decency and visibility.
Blinded by the lights, they say they didn't see
the effects of their tases on his heartbeat,
nor him in distress or gasping, "I can't breathe,"
and pleading, "please, please, save me."

High beams illuminated their reckless behavior
and excessive use of force, his condition graver,
rendering him limp and lifeless from flares of tasers.
Sparks exposing their reflections in the fog of night
and their lack of empathy for his pain and, eventual, loss of life –
they were blinded by the fame and their heads in lights.

A contracted scene, a chase made-for-TV,
Killed a father of two for having on his high beams.
They broke his finger, but he did not scream,

D.B. MAYS

which leads one to speculate that he transcended
not too long after he was apprehended,
as he was unresponsive for at least ten minutes.

Still, the deputies were exonerated in the case,
but Sheriff Chody lost his re-election race
and was charged with tampering, like deleting *Live* tapes.
Texas House Bill 54, Ambler's Law, was introduced,
and *Live PD*, A&E decided that it would no longer produce
because "Live" encouraged PDs to escalate minor pursuits,
especially for people of darker hues.

The *Statesman* reported car chases increased 54%
when *Live PD* featured the county of Williamson,
and detectives "rushed investigations" and warrants,
pushing the lever forward, making situations more intense
by escalating minor offenses for ratings and good content,
obviously, unconcerned about the consequence.

Nothing more hazardous than police who cannot see,
more treacherous than police who lie and deceive,
more dangerous than police who cannot think,
and more inhumane than police who lack empathy
for a fellow human when he's gasping, "I can't breathe,"
and when he cries for his life, pleading "please, save me."

Oh, Javier would need a full beam of light
on that long, dark, and dusky road that night
because their high beams would blight his life
and, eventually and permanently, dim his light.
If there's one thing an experienced driver knows
is when you're alone in the dark, switch from low
to high-beam mode on that long, dark, and dusky road –
At least, that's what I've been told.

THE RUN

for Ahmaud Arbery and other Black people violated "Exercising while Black"

I'm in the aerial phase,
my feet are above the ground
zig zagging from left to right
trying to outrun these clowns.

I shift mid-stance when they advance,
plotting and calculating my best chance.
I see my mark, then make my start,
sprinting short and fast – I dash, they dart.

They box me in, they run me down
No more running. No! I stand my ground!
With my bare hands, I face this klan,
I turn, confront the cowards like the Black man I am.

Bryan strikes me with his truck;
though I'm struck, I still get up
and try to wrestle the gun from McMichael's son.
It's either the barrel of Travis's gauge or George's gun.

No luck, so I swing, and one lands on his head,
as Daddy George stands guard from the pickup bed
yelling and shouting, the whole block can hear,
but no one cares that I'm alone out here.

It's the middle of the day, I know some are home,
and they see and hear the wrong that's going on.
A Black man is being hunted on their street,
That's why no one calls in help for me.

I hear the shots, three times I'm struck.
I try and try, but I can't get up.
My head is lifted toward the sky,
No pain, I'm riding the runner's high.

Running and running until I can't run no more.
Wearily, I collapse on the graveled bed of Satilla Shores.
The shots should have made my body rock,
but supinator's my gait, so, I don't feel the shock.

My heart is beating fast, breathing has slowed,
foot strikes, toes off, strides long, gait controlled.
I'm a road runner jogging the streets, I'm free.
With the pavement under my feet, I'm at peace.
Run for me.

#IRunWithAhmaud #IRunWithMaud

BEHIND HER EYES

for Sandra Bland and other Black people violated for "Driving while Black"

Eyes vacant, devoid of life,
hanged not once but thrice
by a system that violated your rights,
Waller County who failed to protect your life,
and the grand jury that refused to indict,
the sheriff, staff, and state trooper, alike.
By this outcome, we were not surprised –
They'd already faulted you for your own demise,
although the pictures show you lie with lifeless eyes.
Thus, we question your death being ruled a suicide
and doubt their version of the truth
because it wouldn't make sense for you to do –
after you post "at first, they used a noose,
now all they do is shoot" –
to hang yourself with a makeshift noose ...
No, that doesn't seem or ring true, blue.

Why did they fire the officer for his blatant lies
but not for his role in your loss of life
or for the way he pursued and brutalized
you for allegedly refusing to comply
with his encroachment on your civil rights?
In less than 12 months, he made 1600 stop-and-frisks,
threatened to "light you up" if you continued to *resist*
and then placed you in solitary, though you were high risk.

D.B. MAYS

"How did switching lanes with no signal turn into all this?"
Well, the system is laden with biased laws to justify
the unfathomable ways that Black people die
in the custody of ill-intentioned police
who are given public pardons and legal impunity
for their silencing of people who look like you and me.

Oh, but through these lines and verse, #SandySpeaks,
and through these words that voice unapologetically,
"I'm here to change history," and you have, Sandy, speak.

IN MY OWN WORDS

for Rayshard Brooks and Black people violated "On Parole while Black"

This is a public application and a posthumous interview,
In this court of public opinion, I offer this testimony to you.
Yes, I "was convicted of a crime," and I've done a little time,
but it doesn't mean that what happened to me, to my life, was justified.

I've "done some things wrong," but I "paid my debts to society."
After you read my testimony, perhaps you'll reconsider me.

You see, it was 10:42 p.m. on a Hotlanta Friday night,
I may not have been perfect, but there was value to my life.
I admit, I had a few drinks, and I didn't want a DUI
because I was already on probation and couldn't do no more time.
I was sleeping in my car, unaware that Wendy's called nine
for blocking the drive-through lane, said I was holding up the line.

When Officer #1 tapped on my window, I was sound asleep.
He asked me to move my car, I did, then he began to question me.

He called in for *experience*, and Officer #2 arrived.
He tried to take me into custody for an alleged DUI.
Wait, how are you going to charge me for following the rookie cop's advice?
My car was parked, wasn't going anywhere, you know this isn't right.

I asked to walk to my sister's house nearby, but my request was declined.
Instead, Officer #2 tried to handcuff me but hadn't read the Miranda Rights.
Maybe that MADD Award and the 50 arrests for DUIs
made cop #2 a little overzealous to book me and have me do more time.

Y'all, the thought of being "locked in a room for 23 hours a day" –
It was too "hard to stomach," it was "messing with my mental state."
I broke free because I was tired of being retried for my "mistakes."
Why couldn't the officers see me as human, and just give me a break?

I didn't feel like they "looked at me as an individual," like I had a life,
but I had three beautiful daughters, a loving stepson, and a devoted wife.
They're going to "take me away from my family" and "time with my kids,"
It would "take a while to gain their trust back" and explain the things I did.

So, I got away with a taser after they forced me to the ground.
I ran, returned Officer #2's fire, and missed when I briefly turned around.
Officer #2 knew I wasn't carrying because I let them pat me down.
He still used deadly force; I took three hits and fell to the ground.

I was 18 feet away, no threat, when Office #2 shot me in the back.
They "treated me like an animal" – it's what they do when you're Black.
Officer #1 stood on my shoulders, the pressures of life and, now death,
already weighing me down as Officer #2 kicked
me while I gasped my last breaths.

It's "hard to stomach" doing time, y'all, "when I'm really trying."
Because I ran and had a record, did it justify me dying?

THE CROSSWALK

for Michael Brown and other Black teens violated "Jaywalking while Black"

Eight days out of high school,
the whole world at your feet.
On your way to college, not a coffin,
your mother's son, just a boy at 18.
On the precipice of adulthood,
not a man, not quite yet.
Nonetheless, a perceived threat,
a reality that Black boys cannot forget.

Officer Catch-A-Black: I "felt like a 5-year-old
holding onto Hulk Hogan."
His words, like your death,
illuminate the system is broken.
Even the media emphasize your
height, shape, and size,
always prefacing their portrayals
of your undue and dubious demise.

He stopped you because you jaywalked?
Failure to use the crosswalk warrants 12 shots?
Conflicting accounts of what happened,
but the facts are that there were
six gaping holes in your front,
and you were lying in the street
baking for 4 hours in sweltering heat
by the time his beat was done.

The streets wept for you –
No, the streets wailed.
Public outcry reverberated
for miles and around the globe,
because justice did not prevail.

40 SECONDS

*for Philando Castile and other Black people violated
for the "Right to Bear Arms while Black"*

You were a beautiful human being,
beloved by the students you served
and the staff you supervised in the
school cafeteria where you worked.

You were Mr. Phil, the one who
ensured that no student ate alone
and paid lunch debts, concerned that
children did not have food at home.

You were a kind and considerate soul
who was lauded by school staff
for remembering every name and allergy.
A genteel spirit; still, your life ended tragically.

After 49 traffic stops,
with most thrown out,
traffic stop number 50
would be the end of your route.

And all it took was 40 seconds
for the cop to give you unclear directives,
draw and discharge his weapon
in a four-year-old girl's presence
because he said that he felt threatened.

D.B. MAYS

Officer: License and registration
You: *Sir, ... I have a firearm on me.*
Officer's hand is on his holster,
he's full of nervous energy.
Officer: *Okay, don't reach for it then.*
You: *I'm, I, I was reaching for ...*
Officer is losing control,
he can't hear you anymore.
Officer: *Don't pull it out!*
You: *I'm not pulling it out.*
Your girlfriend: *He's not.*
Officer: *Don't pull it out!*

Bang, bang, bang, bang!
Pop, pop, pop!
Seven shots, five to the body,
and two pierced the heart.

And all it took was 40 seconds
for the cop to give you unclear directives,
draw and discharge his weapon
in a four-year-old girl's presence
because he said that he felt threatened.

Something is wrong with the world
when a trained cop, a man, full grown
will endanger a little girl's life
to supposedly save his own.

EVERYTHING TO DO WITH RACE

for Quawan "Bobby" Charles and other Black children "Missing while Black"

Where are our children?
Why don't you search?
No sense of urgency, no Amber alert.
To you – what are our children worth?

Certainly not your concern nor your time.
The minutes, hours, and days you let fly by
reduces the likelihood that you will find
our missing Black boys and girls unharmed or alive.

Must use our own resources, and gather our own facts
because we can't depend on the police we fund for that.
If our children were white, and they weren't Black,
you'd search high and low until you got them back.

C'mon, whether you file a missing case
has everything to do with race.

A Black child is missing, something might be going on,
especially since his parents reported him gone too long.
Didn't have the time or resources to ping his phone,
or question the people who took him from his home?

Neighbors say the parties of interest up and moved.
Mayor says the police chief was missing, too.
And all that the people under suspicion have to do
is check in regularly with you? Is this true?

Found him mutilated in a sugar cane field,
Déjà vu, resembling 1955, Emmitt Till.
It's 2020, this can't be real,
but it is because from one century to the next,
the disappearances of our children remain unchecked.

Charged her with delinquency of a minor
and failure to report a missing child,
but not for murder, possession, or endangerment
for the evidence you found?

C'mon, whether she is tried and convicted in this case
has everything to do with race.

STAY HOME TODAY

for Quawan "Bobby" Charles, 2005 – 2020, Iberia Parrish, Louisiana

Stay home today,
Don't go out and play,
Brown boy, you know why.

Beautiful brown eyes,
wide and bright,
quiet, timid, and shy.

Beautiful brown boy,
your mother's joy,
and your father's pride.

Stay home today,
Don't go out and play,
Brown boy, you know why.

Ride on your four-wheeler, ride.
Take My Baby fishing during falling tides.
No, no, it's best you stay inside.

Stay home today,
Don't go out and play,
Brown boy, you know why.

GOD IS WITH US

*for Rev./Senator Pinckney, Charleston Nine, and Black
people violated "Worshipping while Black"*

Mother Emanuel's Charleston Nine were massacred for her role in history,
for being a beacon of light and harboring runaways during the era of slavery,
for leading a slave rebellion under Denmark
Vesey, who was later hanged with 35,
for being a central figure and playing an impactful role during Civil Rights,
for supporting Black Lives Matter and leading rallies in protest for Walter Scott,
for all these reasons, along with race and hate,
Mother's Emanuel Nine were shot.

He researched Emanuel AME, one of the oldest black churches in U.S. History.
So determined to make a footnote for white
supremacy under the flag of confederacy,
on the 193rd anniversary of the uprising in SC, when
supremacists burned her to the ground,
a white supremacist prayed with Mother Emanuel
before gunning her children down.

The irony in his booking was that Officer Slager
was his neighbor in the next cell block.
He was the same officer convicted to two decades for murdering Walter Scott.
Within a two-month span, America managed to produce
a terrorist who wanted to dominate society
and a NCPD officer who shot a man five times in the back
and, thus, was convicted of murder in the second degree.

No one understands how those who survived
could forgive something so unjust,
why community churches leave their doors open to strangers without mistrust,
why the families of those left behind repeat the mantra, "in God we trust."
If you'd ask Mother's Emanuel Nine, they'd likely respond, "God is with us."

DOUBLE JEOPARDY

for Stephon Clark and other Black people violated for
having a "Criminal History while Black"

Don't run, son; son, don't run!
"Show me your hands! Gun, gun, gun!"
Stand still, or they will shoot to kill.
Wait, didn't Philando Castile sit still,
and Andre Hill and Elijah McClain stand up straight?
Maybe you should run, jump the gate, before it's too late.
You know these cops scary, always fearing for their lives.
They see a Black face, and they break out in lies.
You pretty thin, maybe weigh a buck ten soak and wet.
Still, two cops and 20 shots, terrified of the Black threat.

Prosecuted more than once for the same offense,
executed under the pretense of crimes already committed
tried, convicted, sentenced, and served, my word, my word.
Formerly incarcerated and Black means we don't deserve
to have our individual rights upheld by the Fifth Amendment,
our criminal records are subject to unintended consequences
like being shot seven [or was it eight?] times in the back
homicides always legalized, justified when you
have a criminal history while Black.

THE CLUB

for Jordan Davis and other Black boys violated for
"Hanging with Friends while Black"

I don't want to be a member of this club –
a Black body gunned down, perceived as a thug,
a hashtag that trends on social media until the next
Black girl or boy suffers a racially motivated death.

I don't want to be a member of this club –
I want to be in the back seat bumpin hot beats,
ridin out and jammin with my friends again,
but not another victim of a 21st Century lynching.

How is it that anyone who hates the color of my skin
feels empowered to justify bringing my life to an end?

No, I don't want to be a member of this club –
I just want to go home, give my mother and father a hug,
tell them how much I appreciate their support and love,
and how much I wish that they, too, weren't members of this club.

CROSSING JORDAN

*for the parents of Jordan Davis and Black parents who
lost a child for "Being a Teenager while Black"*

Jordan, did you know there's a river in the Middle East called Nahr Al Sharieat?
It flows roughly north to south through the Sea of Galilee.
The Father, the Son, the Holy Spirit, your earthly father, and me
were the five streams that came together to forge the Jordan you would be.

Jordan, do you hear my laments when I kneel on my knees and pray?
I can feel you grieving for me, mother. When you pray, what do you say?

Cross over the river, Jordan, cross into Jericho and leave dry ground.
Cross over the River Jordan to new beginnings and heavenly sounds.
Your wounds are healed, your holes are sealed, bathed in the waters of Jericho,
miracles happen and blessings abound where're my Jordan flows.

Cross over the river, Jordan, like Christ, take refuge from your enemies.
Cross over the River Jordan to wash away your sins and regain your purity.
Cross over the river, Jordan, from earthly bondage, you're finally free.
Cross over the river, Jordan, your life's journey is now complete.

So, flow like the River Jordan, flow to the lyrics of your favorite song.
Flow like the river, Jordan, flow until the stream carries you home.

*I heard your prayers, mother; be at peace because cross the river, I did.
I flowed like the River Jordan, and with my Heavenly Father, I live.*

8 MINUTES AND 46 SECONDS

for George Floyd and other Black people violated
for "Going to the Store while Black"

Huff ... huff ... huff ...
Puff ... puff ... puff ...
Hah ... haaaahh ... haaaahh ...
Mama! ... mama! ... I can't ... gasp.

I ... can't ... breathe.

In the year 2020, May 25, from 8:20 to 8:29,
my entire life flashes before my eyes.
Seems one officer is determined to end my life,
while three others standdown, standby, and watch me die.

I ... can't ... breathe.

Mama! Mama! Please hear my cry!
It's your baby boy ... *I'm going to die ...*
Let me leave this place with dignity,
not another Black victim of police brutality.

I ... can't ... breathe.

Lay me on my chest, ground beneath my cheek,
neck compressed under the weight of Chauvin's knee.
I'm struggling to breathe, please, remove your knee,
Urine released, lying in pee, as I lose control of my faculties.

D.B. MAYS

I ... can't ... breathe.

Three pressing my torso, legs, and neck ... can't feel a thing,
Oh, it hurts ... *my stomach ... my neck ... everything ...*
Please, the knee in my neck, I can't breathe ...
I cry out, appealing to their humanity: *Don't ... kill ... me.*

I ... can't ... breathe.

Their collective failure to protect almost remains unchecked,
while I lie in the street beneath his knee, clearly distressed.
Because of Darnella Frazier, who at 17, bravely films the scene,
the world speaks and moves its feet for me against police brutality.

I ... can't ... breathe.

Labored, short, and shallow breaths –
I'm gasping for air, no oxygen left.
Chauvin, Kueng, Lane, and Thao show no respect,
still, I courteously plead for mercy until my death.

I ... can't ... breathe.

By 8:25, I'm completely out, another Black man down.
Bystander's yell, "he can't move! Get him off the ground!"
Yelling to Chauvin, "You're enjoying it, too. Look at you."
"Your body language explains it!" His actions proof that he knew –

I ... can't ... breathe.

At 8:27, the paramedics finally arrive,
but I have no pulse ... I am no longer alive.
Still, Chauvin will not remove his knee,
even while the medics examine me.

I ... can't ... breathe.

Although the ER pronounced me dead at 9:25,
everyone knew that by 8:29, I had already died.
If weren't for the video, MPD would have likely denied
what really transpired the morn' of May 25 between 8:20 and 8:29.

Baden said, "neck compression affected blood flow to the brain."
The truth is the neck compression made the streets chant my name;
Neck compression relieved of duty, Chauvin, Kueng, Thao, and Lane;
Neck compression made the world march and protest for change.

Can't believe Thao had six complaints, lost a lawsuit for breaking a man's teeth,
Yet, kept his job with MPD; "This is why you don't
do drugs kids," he jested to the streets
while standing guard as Chauvin kneed the life out
of me for *resisting* and an alleged forgery.
Keung and Lane failed miserably as police in their
first week for their failure to intervene,
and, along with Thao, were charged with aiding and
abetting murder in the second degree,
while Chauvin received two counts for second-degree
murder and manslaughter for killing me.

For 8 minutes and 46 seconds, the world will never forget
that Derek Chauvin pressed his knee into my neck,
and the other three officers stood on me or stood by,
while I cried out, "I can't breathe," and eventually died.

I ... can't ... breathe.

......

I was murdered by the cops,
executed on live TV.
For 8 minutes and 46 seconds,
the world watched them suffocate me.

I was murdered by the cops,
pressed their knees into my neck,
and put their weight on my back until
they saw my head drop and felt my heart stop.

Onto the concrete, soaking in the pee,
That eventually released from me,
and all this was after I screamed, "I can't breathe"
and pleaded with them to take their knees off me.

I was murdered by the cops,
while the streets yelled for them to stop,
but they smiled all the while until
they saw my head drop and felt my heart stop.

I was murdered by the cops.

LAST BREATH

for all Black people who "Can't Breathe while Black"

When you took your last breath, we lost our sense of humanity.
When you took your last breath, we descended into insanity.
When you took your last breath, we awakened from a deep sleep,
rose from our slumber, muffled the yawns,
and looked out onto the horizon, but we saw no new dawns.
Only darkness and despair stifled the air, frustrations so muggy and thick,
We ... Can't ... Breathe,
pleading ... gasping ... lungs collapsing beneath the lethal and legal KNEE.

The brutal oppressions and recurring injustices were just too much for we
to believe that there could be anything but no justice, no peace!
When you took your last breath, we wiped disillusionment from our eyes,
cleared the cobwebs of duplicity from the catacombs of our minds,
saw our lifeblood spill onto the streets, resulting in public outcries
to "Defund the police!"
Protests that stilled the faint echo of our collective heartbeat
as we retreated underneath the homicidal knee,
infinitely yielding to eternal sleep.

D.B. MAYS

OFFLINE:
KILLING IN THE DARK

for Korryn Gaines and other Black women violated for "Traffic Tickets while Black"

Beautiful and bold,
if the truth be told.
Make no concessions,
but offer my confession:
I was tired of being mistreated
by the men in blue,
and aggressively pursued because my hue.
Blackness, not the rifle I held
got me killed; my color got me killed.

Because I stood my ground
they would not take me in
like Watson and Frazier –
didn't bother with a negotiator.
But they can talk to white folk all day.
Black standoffs, they don't deescalate.
Why? One can only imagine and speculate
that they were reeling from the message
on my makeshift license plate:

Any government official who compromises
this pursuit of happiness and right to travel (mine)
will be held criminally responsible and fined,
as this is a natural freedom and right.

Yeah, at the traffic stop, you were pretty peeved,
and determined you were going to come get me.
At the time that I die, I will be number nine –
the ninth Black woman in 2016 killed by 9.
Forcing your way in my home with a warrant to serve
You ain't coming in here, ya heard? On my word.
You better leave and head outside on that protect and serve.
I'm Bmore, born and raised, I'm holding it down.
Have all day to protect my son, I'm standing my ground.

Six hours later, wouldn't stand down,
filmed it live until Facebook suspended my accounts,
helping Baltimore CPD, under the cover of night,
make an unlawful entry and take my life.
Wouldn't let my mother negotiate at the scene,
although she fervently pleaded to intervene
to prevent you from harming my baby and me.
I'm at peace. ... They've been quiet awhile, so they
plotting to come in here and disturb the peace.

Knew my five-year-old son was in the line of fire,
but it didn't stop you from endangering his life
Shot my little boy in the cheek and a limb,
then wouldn't let my family see or comfort him.
Black women commonly killed by police for minor offenses,
but the police are rarely held accountable for the consequences.
In fact, the one who killed me got promoted and stripes.
although two civil juries believed he violated our civil rights
and awarded $38 million to my family for the loss of my life.

Holding my child,
I was gunned down.
No negotiator, no empathy,
no regard for my son and me.
When the cop fired shots, assassinating me,
I cradled my baby as I drifted to peace,
I cradled my baby while he mourned for me.

Don't worry, my son, my daughter, *I'm at peace.*
I'm in my home. I ain't trying to hurt nobody, release.

CHOKED OUT

*for Eric Garner and other Black people violated for
"Selling Untaxed Goods while Black"*

Having been arrested thirty times since 1980,
maybe, just maybe, that was ENOUGH for me.
After having a cop conduct a cavity search on me,
put HIS FINGERS in my RECTUM in the middle of the street
with neighbors ... strangers walking by LOOKING at me,
I wanted to be treated with HUMAN decency,
and I was TIRED of being deprived of my DIGNITY –
so, maybe, just maybe, that was ENOUGH for me.

CHOKED out by the system, CHOKED out by the cops,
I was TIRED of being a VICTIM, I wanted it to STOP.
Already out on bail for the same offense,
continually harassing me for untaxed cigarettes,
here comes NYPD BELITTLING me AGAIN,
so, I STOOD UP for my RIGHTS, said, I AM a MAN.
Same cop, same block, I wanted it to STOP,
but I was CHOKED out by the system and CHOKED out by the cops.

I can't breathe. You're choking me.
I can't breathe. You're choking me.
I can't breathe. You're choking me.
I can't breathe. You're choking me.
I can't breathe. You're choking me.
I can't breathe. You're choking me.
I can't breathe. You're choking me.

D.B. MAYS

I can't breathe. You're choking me.
I can't breathe. You're choking me.
I can't breathe. You're choking me.
I can't breathe. You're choking me.

One minute ... Two minutes ... Three minutes ...
Four minutes ... Five minutes ... Six minutes ... Seven minutes ...
was the exact length of time that I lie outside,
face down, on the ground, unconscious, until medics arrived.
The county medical examiner ruled my death a homicide,
and the autopsy read, "compression of neck,
compression of chest ..." causes of death.

NO GOOD DEED

For Ramsey Orta and other people violated for "Filming the Police while Black"

I didn't physically die,
but I literally died inside
because the NYPD ensured
my personal demise
for opening the whole world's eyes,
and shedding a light on how the police
abuse Black lives and violate Black rights.

Because I filmed the incident,
they preserved a special spot for me
down at the 120th Precinct.
Now, I'm not portraying a life of innocence,
was on a wayward path at 13 and walked
a curved one since,
but for filming what happened to Eric Garner,
I consider it time well spent.

My video showed the last moments of Eric's life
an officer's arm around his neck, pressing his windpipe,
Eric repeating 11 times, "I can't breathe,"
officers ignoring him, pushing his face into the concrete,
and the same officer holding his grip until Eric went limp.
Because my video went viral, NYPD retaliated for exposing them.

D.B. MAYS

Cops followed me every day since Eric died,
trailing me in unmarked cars and, to fright,
shining bright lights in my house every night,
and arresting me multiple times
on trumped up charges and false crimes.
Yeah, they were determined that I would do time
for exposing the darkness behind their precious blue line.

In retaliation, they threatened, beat, and poisoned me
while I was at Rikers in the spring of 2015,
then boxed me in, had to cop a plea when I was out on bail.
If I refused, they were going to send my mother to jail.
What son would risk sending his mother to prison?
I decided to do the time for the life I'd been living.
But the real tragedy is what they did to me
during those years I was locked up from 2015 to 2020.

There's nothing uncommon about what happened to me,
harassing people who film them is a pattern for police.
Intimidating and pursuing, hoping to discourage and silence,
they continually target citizen journalists who film police violence.
In fact, the people who filmed Castile's, Gray's, and Sterling's deaths
suffered similar harassment and faced multiple arrests.

The irony is the medical examiner ruled Eric's death a homicide –
They killed him, I filmed him, but I'm the only one doing time!
Even though they took me away from my wife and kids
and took five years of my life while I was doing that bid,
Although I'd rather the video never existed, and Eric had lived,
I still have no regrets about what I did, I would film it again
because they deserved to be exposed for killing my friend.

For my video and testimony to be valid, my record must be squeaky clean,
but the same isn't required of the officers who are policing me?
Bordering prosecutorial misconduct for releasing my criminal record to TV,
but they fail to mention that Pantaleo's record was far from pristine.

For false arrests and abuse, he had two civil rights lawsuits in 2013,
one for allegedly searching and making black men strip naked on the street.
Though the men's charges were dismissed, and Pantaleo killed E,
the NYPD didn't fire him until 2019?

While they released me early under the Covid provision,
until January 2022, I remain under court supervision.
Understand that a lot can happen between now and then,
especially with the lawsuits I have pending against them.
Again, I don't feign to be innocent or your model citizen,
but we all know that my real crime was filming the incident.
I've committed some crimes, but the police did, too,
and my viral video is proof of what they do to people of a darker hue.

HUNTING SEASON

for Casey Goodson and other Black people violated
"Entering Your Home while Black"

From his pulpit he preached
that it is a "righteous release"
to exercise his "use of force"
on people who look like me.
His job, he said, is to "hunt people,"
emphasizing how he "loves it," it's "great."
On that fatal day I would learn too late
that he was the predator and I the prey.
He spent all day glassing my terrain,
searching but drew a blank hunting wild game.

Weather was fairly cool and bright,
the steady December breeze must've been just right
for that old hound to pick up the scent
of my concealed weapon and carry permit.
Either he had a scope mounted atop his rifle,
or we can go with logic – he was homicidal.

Oh, Charlie, you really are a sly old fox,
using my granny's home as a rabbit box,
the dry set for you to trap and snare
a fine human specimen, something rare,
a Black male target for your trophy hunt.
Truth is he did an old run and gun
driving through my habitat midday

for an ornament to mount in his display.
Jump shooting, taking me by surprise,
shooting from the field, he laydown blind.
Game wounded, he caught me from behind,
five follow-up shots in the back, one in my hind.

Then, he cut and run, hunter-gathering lies,
wanting all to hear how he captured his prize.
Returning to base camp with tall tales, the way hunters do,
about the dangers he faced in the act of pursuit,
how his prey goaded him, taunted, and teased,
how he had no choice but to kill his seize
at the expense of racial balance and morality.

They believed him, too, because he's camouflaged in blue.
Hiding behind the badge, he easily disguised the truth.
But something about his story didn't ring true –
Granny said I was coming through the door
with sandwiches in hand and then fell to the floor.
For the number of hits that I took to the back,
there is no way he felt threatened or attacked.

When questioned, the babbling hound made no sense,
laying a drag for the hunting party to follow, an artificial scent
that lead them to more questions than answers about his assail.
Desperate, he spent weeks hunting his backtrail,
trying to retrace his steps, to justify his strike,
his sit and wait, stalking prey, and slaughtering human life.

This was the opening meet, a sport-kill, no other reason,
I was merely Black game, the start of hunting season.

But we're at trophic level, occupy the same position in the chain,
Sport-killing season is over; on the hunt, and we're not the game.

Tally-ho, brothers and sisters, tally-ho!
Must rid the system of sport-killers high and low,
along with bloodhounds and sly foxes, they must go.
Tally-ho, brothers and sisters! Tally-ho!

SEASON'S GREETINGS

for Andre Hill and other Black people violated for
"Holidaying with Friends while Black"

There was holiday cheer in the air,
now the mistle toe is hung in despair.
The wintry breeze was crisp and clean,
then shots rang out, leaving smoke rings.
Bullet shells hang from my limbs,
suspended from branches like ornaments.
The powdered pavement is cold and icy.
Like snowflakes, tears fall, sticking to my cheeks.
Red and blue lights outline my figure decoratively
and flash brightly like bulbs on a Christmas tree.
The holiday punch spills from my cavities,
a swill of red flows from my head to my feet,
making me a frozen, red snow angel in the street.
Carolers in blue gather, but none extend charity.
For 5 minutes and 11 seconds, they hum but not to me.
Silver bells chime as I lie dying,
offering Christmas greetings to the police.

D.B. MAYS

BLOODIED & BRUISED

for Ronald Green and other Black people "Brutalized by Police while Black"

Louisiana State Trooper Chris Hollingsworth:
I beat the ever-livin fuck out of him.
Choked him and everything else
trying to get him under control.
We finally got him in handcuffs
when a third man got there.
And the son of a bitch was still fightin.
They were wrestlin with him, tryin to hold him down.
He was spittin blood everywhere.
Then, all of a sudden, he just went limp.

That's what Louisiana troopers did to me after a high-speed chase.
Dragged me face down across the pavement,
and beat me bloody, leaving deep bruises on my face.
No surprise I went into cardiac arrest; they repeatedly stun gunned me.
In distress when they pinned me to the ground with their steel-booted feet.
Did you know that long before I was hogtied, I had complied,
put my hands up in submission and offered my contrition.
"I'm sorry," I repeated to the members of the party, "I'm sorry."

I'm sorry if this description is too graphic, but this was the scene.
Imagine my family watching the video of the brutality inflicted on me.
Hey, hey now. This happened to me, it didn't happen to you,
and in death, as in life, I have the right to speak my own truth.

Friend, this is the America we live in.
The one that continually brutalizes her Black daughters and sons,
while many march, protest, and pray for this era to end,
It takes a break ever now and then, but the new age of rage has only just begun.

ROUGH RIDE

for Freddie Gray and other Black people violated "In-Custody while Black"

Presses the gas pedal one, two, three times.
Vroom ... vroom ...vroom ... vroom!
The engine roars before the abrupt start,
then the wagon drives fast and loose.
Body involuntarily lunges forward,
but I muster all the strength
to prevent my descent.
Although my limbs are aching –
"folded" like playdoh during the arrest –
manage to force my torso upright,
and press my back against the metal wall,
hoping it will wrap itself around me
and secure me to this metal seat
because I'm handcuffed, no seatbelt
and cannot protect myself with shackled feet.

Swerving and turning so erratically
that whiplash is an understatement.
Swoosh! Swish! Swoosh! Swish!
My neck jerks wildly from right to left,
backward and forward, up and down.
My head seems to be spinning around.
Bobble, bobble, bobble. Wobble, wobble.
Whirr, whirr, whirr! Whish, whish, whish!
Soooo dizzy, sooooo nauseous,
choking on vomit that's stuck in my esophagus.

Out-brake. Eerrrk! Boom! Thud!
No safety barrier for me.
Metal wall betrays me, releases me,
and cruelly tosses me to its neighbor,
who fails to catch me.
So, I fall hard to the floor,
slamming against the metal sheet,
feels like the floor of a wrestling ring.
Argh! My body is screaming from the pain.
Everything is rattling inside my head.
The engine restarts. Stop the motor.
I want it to be over.

Bump, bump, bump, bump! Smack!
Something inside me cracks,
and I feel my neck snap.
As I'm flung violently from one end to the other,
I know that I am never going to recover.
Feels like the end as the wheels spin,
as the wheels spin, it feels like the end.

By the time I cross the finish line,
everything in me is broken inside.
The medical examiner rules my death a homicide,
noting sustained injuries to the head and spinal cord,
and three fractured vertebrae, 80% severed at the neck.
He concluded all were consequences of a rough transport.

Having drifted a week between this place and the next,
I finally succumb to my injuries and welcomed my death.

D.B. MAYS

GOLDILOCKS

for Botham Jean and other Black people violated
for "Relaxing at Home while Black"

Once upon a time in Dallas, there lived a man who loved to sing.
He had a big heart and, so, volunteered his time
helping vulnerable communities.
A graduate of Harding, he excelled in accounting
and was on the partnership track at PwC.
At the end of long days, he liked to settle down and enjoy a tub of ice cream.
That's what he was doing, the night of the shooting
– eating a bowl and watching TV.

"Open up! Let me in! Let me in!" the neighbors heard on the floor,
but the man did not hear Goldilocks making an unlawful entry at his door.
Pretty soon, he came upon the female intruder who illegally entered his home,
but she stood looking at him as if he was the person doing wrong.
When Goldilocks burst inside, the man caught such a terrible fright
because there was a woman in his living room,
holding a gun, and threatening his life.

"Let me see your hands!" she reportedly commanded,
her finger itching on the trigger.
Caught by surprise, the man blinked his eyes but
didn't recognize her as an authority figure.
Goldilocks was not wearing her blue costume;
thus, the man was likely confused.
He may have yelled in response, "Hey! Get out of
my place! Who in God's name are you?"

Goldilocks thought she would escape her fate because she wears a blue costume.
Later, when she told her story to a judge and jury,
they didn't believe her story to be true.

Goldilocks, this level is too high, you're on level three, and this is four.
Goldilocks, this is unit 1498, there's a lighted sign on the door.
Goldilocks, this doormat is too red, and there is only concrete outside yours.
Goldilocks, this home is too messy, and your home is super neat.
Goldilocks, this home is too smoky, and you say you don't smoke weed.

"Ahhh, this home is just right," Goldilocks sighed unreasonably,
although the door was supposedly opened, and Goldilocks didn't use her key.
Goldilocks supposedly realized her errors when
the dead man was lying at her feet.
And that's why Goldilocks is serving 10 years for murder in the first degree.

Amber Guyger was a brown-haired woman when she killed Botham Jean.
When did Guyger become Goldilocks? By her
second court visit, she was blonde.

THE END

INTRUDER

for Atatiana Jefferson and other Black people violated "Babysitting while Black"

We hear noises outside our window.
Someone is in our yard whom we don't know.
I could make a formal petition for him to leave,
and maybe on his own volition, he'll retreat.
I can't take that chance, my nephew and I are alone,
and should this intruder make his way into our home,
there are so many ways that he could violate this space.
No, I have to keep us safe.

So, I draw my gun, but I'm blinded by the light
shining at me from the other side where the intruder hides.
Before I can make out what the voice is saying, I am hit
The screams of my nephew, I'll never forget

Officer #1, conducting a welfare check at the scene,
after peeping through the window, fired the fatal shot at me,
without announcing himself to me or providing any identity.
He jumped the fence and, after a glance inside,
shot into my home and ended my life, never thinking to verify
if I was the person whom he was called to protect on his welfare check.

THE LITTLE GIRL ON LILLIBRIDGE STREET

For Aiyana Stanley Jones and other brown-skinned
girls violated "Sleeping while Black"

There is an aimless squatter, but the duplex looks abandoned.
The splintered porch boards and dangling shutters are badly battered.
With the exception of the moth-eaten sofa, the rooms are barren,
but a single occupant sits on the sofa, swinging blood-spattered legs
from beneath a faded Hannah Montana gown that is torn and tattered.
Every night, around 12:40 am, she shakes uncontrollably with dread
and tears spill from her sad brown eyes because,
once again, she realizes she's dead.
Night after night, she dodges a flash-bang grenade but does not survive the shot
in reel and real time by *First 48* and, in real life, a bullet to the neck by a cop.
She futilely presses her little bloodstained hand to
her neck, but the bleeding never stops.
Tormented, her wail has no outlet because, where her
larynx used to be, there's a gaping hole.
And where there was once a bright-eyed, little, brown-
skinned girl, there is now a restless soul
who has nowhere to go and, with each passing year, does not grow old;
There is no birthday cake, no candles to blow, just a
grim reminder that she remains 7-years-old.

THE DRUM ROLL HOME

for Corey Jones and other Black people violated "Stranded while Black"

Yes, I am my brother's keeper,
and for you, my brother, I speak
through these lowly lines of poetry
to reverently record your life's release
and, most importantly, to elevate your memory.

Waiting for roadside assistance, the stranded man
is approached by an ominous, dark-windowed van
from whence an interloper ascends issuing commands.
Presuming it a ruse, the lone motorist is taken aback
by the intruder, clad in a T-shirt, jeans, and baseball cap,
who screams nonsensical demands like, "Hold up your hands!"
Feeling unsafe when the trespasser encroaches on his personal space,
the marooned traveler looks for an opportunity to get away.
So, he runs along the shoulder of I-95 in the dark of night
to nowhere or no one in particular but determined to protect his life.

It would seem that his concerns were justified,
having been shot six times and hit in the body thrice
by the interloper who failed to state his purpose or identify
that he was, indeed, a policeman; about this, he'd repeatedly lie,
which is why former officer, Raja was convicted and is serving 25.
Though the motorist received justice for his tragic end that night,
justice would not undo the harm, nor would it restore his life.

That's why near the southbound exit of the
PGA, in the wee hours of the morn',
a drummer clicks his pitch-paired sticks, then hits, and plays a mournful song
that travels along a deserted road, resting beneath an aimless soul
who, to the familiar beat of the boom boom boom, sways and moves
his arms, hips, and feet in rhythm with the reggae tune and the drum groove,
and dances his way to Heaven's gates where the
angels perform a slow drum roll,
the trumpets play, and his mother sings greetings,
welcoming her beloved boy home.

D.B. MAYS

MIAMI "305" LOVE

*for Trayvon Martin and other Black boys violated for
"Walking in the Neighborhood while Black"*

You were so much more than the system and media portrayed you to be.
Seventeen like Brandy, you just wanted to be free,
a beautiful Black boy, allowed to be a teen, and do adolescent things
without your digital footprint fully defining you as a human being.
Know you loved Pac, DMX, and Mystikal, think
you'll appreciate the references.
Because I admire you and Pac, too, I wanted to show deference.

Since your death, life's illuminated systemic and societal hypocrisies,
like the many excuses made for white nationalists and members of the GOP
for their racist rhetoric, racial violence, and racial biases,
but we're told to accept their insincere apologies,
and not judge them for lapses in judgement or the ill ways they behave,
or the discriminatory actions and insensitive statements they make.
Say we can't characterize them by the few things they say or do,
but it is precisely what the justice system and society did to you.

Your social media supposedly revealed the truth about you,
providing the courts of justice and public opinion proof
that you were a thug who viciously beat a grown man,
not the unarmed, frightened child who defended your life until your tragic end,
not the brave, brown boy, who at age nine, saved your father's life,
not your mother's loving son, a devoted brother, and a Chief for life,
not the boy who played football, enjoyed sports, and loved playing video games,

not the student who took ownership of your learning
because you wanted to fly planes,
not the teen who, while attending school, completed
an aviation program in 8 weeks,
and not the industrious youth who washed cars,
babysat, and cut grass to earn money.

Black boy taught to *watch ya self* when you're in
danger and approached by a clown.
Black boy, they said *he could but wish you would*,
you're not allowed to stand your ground.
I imagine you had no choice but to *get it on the floor*. If not, *how's it going down?*
I imagine you told him that if he ain't *start nothin*, it wouldn't *be nothin*,
but since he started *somethin*, it was *gone be somethin*.
The Catch-22 in what you could to do is why we
talk to our sons who look like you.
Life has us all so confused, what's a Black boy
supposed to do when approached by a fool?

Like Pac said, "for every dark night, there's a brighter day,"
and he was right, "real eyes realize real lies" – we learned that from your case.
Because you flashed a gold grill, they used that and more to justify being killed.
Interestingly, I rocked gold teeth as an educator; I'm just keeping it real,
and I was still a great teacher while I was #TeachingItTrill.
When the media snapped pictures, I rocked a Fendi scarf and flashed my grill,
so, the city could see that people who look like us are free to be *who we be*
and look like anything in the world that we want to be
while defying racial stereotypes and cultural biases.

I want you to know, Black boy from the 305, that you did nothing wrong.
I hope you're proudly rockin your grill, hoodie, and headphones
while bumpin your favorite Mystikal, DMX, and Tupac rap songs.

So many tears have been shed for you, but there have been positive *changes* too.
Your parents are activists, started a foundation, and wrote a book about you.
They are doing their best to honor you; I hope they
picture you rollin with Pac like I do.
FMU awarded you a posthumous degree, too,
so, now you're qualified to *fly high*
One more road to cross, and you crossed it. Like
Pac, you're a legend, you'll never die.

Please, say a *Hail Mary* for your brothers and
sisters left out here in these streets.
Black boy from the 305, always a Carol City Chief,
rest in power, rest in rap, rest in peace.

RACIALIZED MEDICAL ABUSE

*for Dr. Susan Moore, Kira Johnson, and other Black people
violated seeking "Healthcare while Black"*

In 2020, COVID-19 swept the world, devastating this country,
reportedly impacting the Black community disproportionately.
At five times the hospitalizations, and three times the mortality,
COVID-19 highlighted enduring racial disparities and inequities
in the healthcare system that treats Black lives through biased eyes
and believes that Blacks do not feel pain to the same degree as whites.
Thus, for the same illness or surgery, doctors prescribe pain killers
and administer certain treatments less frequently for blacks than whites.

One of its causalities was a physician who, although facing imminent death,
shared her experience with medical racism from the
hospital bed and with her last breath,
describing that while hospitalized with COVID-
19 and because of the skin she was in,
she was denied the treatment that she requested and effective pain medicine.
She did not receive the antiviral that would relieve
her pain and help her to breathe;
she needed to prove her condition before her physician would provide her relief.
She added that the medical team repeatedly dismissed
her concerns, despite her expertise,
and treated her with disdain for her professional background and self-advocacy.

The hospital seemingly implied that she was a
difficult patient and too complex to treat,
suggesting that for Blacks to be shown compassion,
Blacks must acquiesce, not beseech.
"I put forward, and I maintain: If I were white,
I wouldn't have to go through that."
Studies show that inequality has become the healthcare
system's standard of care for Blacks.
"My doctor made me feel like I was a drug addict,
and he knew I was a physician;"
Yet, he still thought me incapable of effectively communicating my own condition
and unqualified, despite my degree and experience,
of making a sound, professional decision.

COVID-19 isn't the only medical tragedy spreading
like a virus in the Black community.
Blacks are also disproportionately affected by maternal mortality and morbidity.
The frequency that infant and pregnant fatalities
happen for Black women is an absurdity.
America is the only developed country where, for
pregnant mothers, the death rate is rising,
and each year 50,000 experience serious complications
while at least 700 are dying.
Black pregnant women across socioeconomic and
education levels are at the top of that list
because Black women's concerns and health issues
are often ignored, dismissed, or missed.

Even more egregious than that, Black mothers are
three to four times more likely than whites
to lose their Black babies to premature deaths and to lose their own Black lives,
leaving their children without Black mothers and
their partners without Black wives.
Why are Black women 243% more likely to die from pregnancy or delivery?

Based on statistics, it is not unreasonable to
conclude that Black maternal morbidity
is, to some extent, a consequence of health inequities,
medical biases, and racial disparities.

Black people are policed in medicine by white coats
like they are policed by blue in life –
When Black people say we're hurting, or we can't
breathe, white coats assume it is a lie,
taking approaches to care that cause Blacks to agonize,
have a diminished quality of life, or die.
While they may provide the standard of care, it's not
the high-quality care afforded to whites.

If medical professionals believe that Black people
are prone to disease and poor health,
it makes it impossibly difficult for them to value
Black humanness and treat Blacks well.
Because Black people have been historically
subjected to racialized medical abuse,
Black people have a deep distrust of the healthcare
system that is valid and based on truths,
like the *psychiatric diagnosis of drapetomania* that
resulted in amputations of enslaved runaways,
akin to the diagnosis of excited delirium used to justify
in-custody injuries and deaths today.
Blacks have not forgotten the Tuskegee experiments,
Henrietta Lacks, and government
sanctioned sterilization of Blacks from slavery through the present century,
or universities using Black bodies to experiment and teach,
with little to no regard for Black humanity.

Thus, it should be no surprise that Blacks regard the
coronavirus vaccine with great cynicism,
considering the well-documented, multiple-century
Black experience with medical racism.

D.B. MAYS

There will be little improvements in patient satisfaction
or practitioner-patient interaction,
while healthcare profession diversity data continue to
show a significant gap in representation,
and statistics that do not reflect society: Black citizens
make up 13.4% of the U.S. population,
but Black people account for less than 5% of
practicing physicians in the entire nation.
Until the healthcare system and its providers address
and eradicate medical abuse and racism,
for which Blacks are disproportionately and, too
often fatally, the primary victims,
the Black community has valid reasons to continue
its mistrust of the healthcare system.

DELIRIUM

for Elijah McClain and other Black people violated
for "Walking Home while Black"

"My name is Elijah McClain.
That's my house. I was just going home.
I'm an introvert. I'm just different," I tried to explain
when four officers detained and restrained me for doing nothing wrong.
This is a case of mistaken identity, I thought. I told them, "I have my ID.
I have no gun. I don't do that stuff. I don't do any fighting."
They could not have understood me because they treated me so cruelly.
Maybe I offended them? I tried to apologize: "I'm
so sorry. Why are you attacking me?
I don't even kill flies! I don't eat meat, but I don't
judge people ... who does eat meat."
They ignored my pleas, handcuffed and held me on the ground forcibly,

"Ow, that really hurts! You are all very strong."
"Teamwork makes the dream work," but I'm only 140 pounds and all alone.
It's been nearly 15 minutes and there are three of you on top of me.
I'm sobbing uncontrollably, but not one provides me any relief
or shows any human decency, although I say over and over, "I can't breathe,"
and repeatedly regurgitate my snacks and iced
tea, getting it all over them and me.
"Oh, I'm sorry, I wasn't trying to do that. I just can't breathe correctly,"
but they put me in a chokehold, anyway, compressing
my neck and carotid arteries.
Before I lose consciousness, I manage to say to the
police, who treated me so brutally:

D.B. MAYS

"I'm sorry. I'm so sorry. I can't breathe. Forgive me.
All I was trying to do was become better. I will do it. I will do anything.
You are beautiful, and I love you. Try to forgive me."

This is what the police did to a 23-year-old unarmed kid
who was *gentle, intellectually gifted, eccentric*, different,
a *spiritual seeker, vegan* and *musician* who performed at animal shelters,
believing his music gave them peace, and he was their protector;
a massage therapist who was lauded for being "the sweetest, purest" guy
and whose friends say he wouldn't "set a mousetrap" or "harm a fly."
This is how 9-1-1 protected and served a defenseless *peacemaker* –
pumped him with ketamine after cutting off the blood flow to his brain,
sedating him for *excited delirium*, but it was their quartet who was insane.
Brain dead, he suffered cardiac arrest and three
days later was sent to the undertaker.

By the time they had protected and served, Elijah had endured a world of hurt,
because, for them, his Black life had no value, to them it had no worth.
To commemorate their crime against humanity, they stood at his memorial site
photographing themselves mimicking his death
and mocking the loss of his human life.

AMERICA'S CHILD

for Tamir Rise, Tajai Rice, and all Black children
who are violated "Playing while Black"

No story written by her wayward sons can possibly explain,
unless America has gone absolutely insane –
and if she has, we need to provide urgent medical help
because she is a danger to others and herself –
how she justifies the murder of her 12-year-old son,
a little brown boy, for allegedly waving, in a park, a toy gun.

No empathy for his sissy, who at 14, understandably screams
from the shock of witnessing her little brother's body
be rocked twice by real bullets and flood real blood,
but the police show her no sympathy, tackling her hard
before handcuffing and throwing her into the back of the patrol car.
The boys in blue provided no aid to your little brown boy as he lay dying,
and left his grieving sister, your daughter, alone, handcuffed, and crying.

Made your elder daughter, their mother, choose between the
Black girl whom your blue sons improperly detained,
or accompanying your dying Black son to the hospital
and, later, attending to his remains.
Similar to slavery if the enslaved were ever given a choice –
Which one do you want us to sell or keep, the girl or the boy?
Yeah, your mental state is unquestionably unstable, America, you're insane.
You need to be committed for racial violence and the centuries of Black pain,

especially, the Black genocide you perform under
the guise of legalese and decrees.
You're an unfit mother who fails to protect her darker
children from brutalities and casualties.

We learned much later that the police cruiser never came to a complete stop.
So, the officer really couldn't ascertain that the boy
was a boy before he fired the shots,
or that the gun he was allegedly reaching for at his
waist was a toy gun, replica Airsoft.
Even the judge was "thunderstruck by how quickly"
the boy's life was ended by the cop.
Independence had already deemed the same officer
"emotionally unstable and unfit for duty."
If Cleveland had done its due diligence, there would
never have been a Tamir Rice shooting.

BALLAD OF ALTON STERLING

for Alton Sterling and other Black people violated for "Selling Media while Black"

In a parking lot in Baton Rouge down on North Forster Drive
the levees of injustice gave way after midnight on July five.
The CD Man stopped spinning; his songs would play no more,
for an anonymous call rang in a threat at the convenience store.

But before his score would end, rambunctious laughter filled the air.
His baritone resounded, bellowing the goods he had to share
to the gathering of familiar faces who were seemingly unaware
of the ill-fated occurrence that would soon happen there.

Sterling, the CD Man, would be taken entirely by surprise
by flashes of red and blue illuminating the dark and starless sky.
Unbeknownst to Alton Sterling, he would make his final sell
and meet his tragic end, an event he could not foretell.

Two white officers confronted Sterling in the lot of the Triple Mart
Shop owner Abdullah said "the cops were aggressive from the start.
Sterling did not wield his gun; so, he did not deserve to be shot."
Yet, the familiar police refrain would end with Sterling's heart at full stop.

Cell phone videos illustrated that Sterling was confounded by the cops.
"What did I do?" he asked incessantly, and the cops seemingly blew their tops.
His would-be murderers seized him, then thrust him toward a silver sedan.
They said that they felt threatened although they were two against one man.

They gave ambiguous orders: "don't move" but "put your hands on the car."
"All right, all right," Sterling complied; still, they pinned down both his arms.
Officer A tasered Sterling with a stun gun before tackling him to the ground,
while Officer B drew his weapon, eager to release a couple of rounds.
He pressed the barrel to Sterling's head, then aimed the gun at his chest
while yelling, "Don't f**ng move, or I'll shoot" followed by a series of expletives.

Officer B continued to scream threats, "I'm going to shoot ... if you move!"
Sterling was pinioned and immobile, bystanders' videos would later prove.
With the body cameras dislodged, and the scene out of public view,
the subsequent sequence of events was easier to misconstrue.

One officer conveniently shouted to passersby near and far, "He's got a gun!"
With that calculated claim, Mr. Sterling, father of five and beloved son
would play his final song, then an affrettando conducted by killer cops,
and a cacophony of casualty quickly grew to a crescendo of six shots.
Every bullet deftly landed, seemingly death was the officer's aim.
The autopsy would confirm that Sterling was shot at point-blank range.
Standing before the slain Sterling, Officer B spewed profanities,
calling him a "stupid mother[sucker]" to rationalize his insanity.

The executioners had to think quickly to justify ending Alton's life
on the morning of July 5, the time signature read 12 and the bar 45.
Complicit in the murder, Officer A pulled an object from Alton's pants pocket.
Thereafter, the alleged gun in Alton's possession would become a central topic
of a corrupt investigation that would continue for 11 months
but not before the streets of Baton Rouge were completely overrun.

The police and legal system would justify the catastrophic events.
Thus, the banks of Baton Rouge would rise in discontent,
and the outdated levee system that drowned New Orleans
would do the same to Baton Rouge whose streets burst at the seams.

As protests surged and courts dropped sandbags to plug the levee break,
nothing would stop the flow of frustration or keep the police at bay.
Its levees of justice were short and weak, compromised by bureaucracy,
because these iniquitous acts were continually upheld by polluted agencies.

DA Hillar Moore eventually recused himself from the Alton Sterling case,
Citing he knew Officer B's parents, former cops, so AG Landry took his place.
Nearly one year after Governor John Edwards turned the case over to the DOJ,
Louisiana AG Jeff Landry would announce the decision of the state:
The DOJ will not file criminal charges against the two white officers involved.
On the murder of Alton Sterling, the protestors declared, "It's not resolved!"

Landry further maintained that Alton Sterling did indeed resist arrest,
although videos showed Officer A pinning Sterling
down and B shooting six bullets in his chest.
"Let us not forget," Landry cautioned to those whom he knew would object,
"That use of force requires officers to reasonably perceive a threat."

Since Sterling was immobile, critics argued that he was no danger, in fact;
the shooting was another example of excessive
force against someone who is Black.
To the DOJ, it was a lawful arrest, to the people, an immoral act.
One only needs to look from the 1400s to 2000s for examples of that.

How could someone resist arrest if the Miranda Rights weren't read?
Did the officers read the Rights before they shot
him, as he bled, or after he was dead?
New East Baton Rouge police chief, Paul, had no answer, but he apologized
for the hiring of Officer B and the lies that led to Alton's eventual demise.
Chief Paul unveiled Officer B's history of unnecessary use of force
and incidents of insubordination and abuse noted in his personnel report.
One officer told his superior that Officer B would eventually kill someone
Because he was always looking for a fight and eager to brandish his gun.

Chief Paul explained that although Officer A did
help wrestle Sterling to the ground,
of the six shots that entered Sterling's body, Officer A hadn't fire one round.
So, Officer B was fired from the force, but Officer A retained his position.
Both had been on paid administrative leave while awaiting the decision.

Most believed that the investigation was a farce from the
start because there would be no prosecution,
and for the loss of Alton's life, his family would receive no restitution.
Although the police used excessive force and the father of five died that day,
four years later, Metro Council decided that $5
million was excessive and refused to pay.
The distraught mother of Alton's children would go on to say,
"They killed him in cold blood ... they took a human away."

Once more, the tides of racial tension overflowed in Baton Rouge's streets.
Though a judgement was rendered, peaceful protests would last for weeks.
Police responded wearing military gear and wielding weapons of war;
Protestors questioned the purpose of government — who was justice for?

Because the crowds would not disperse, mass arrests of protestors ensued.
Most arrests were unlawful and often brutal, resulting in a class-action lawsuit.
The local and state governments were determined to win the fight,
but a federal judge awarded $1000 to each
protestor for violating their civil rights.

Although the crowds have receded, justice has not prevailed –
not for the children of Alton Sterling nor for Sterling, the assailed.
Still, somewhere down in Baton Rouge, the music plays again,
the notes are high, songs full of life, but not for Sterling, the CD man.

In a parking lot on N. Forster Drive where Alton Sterling lost his life,
the miscarriage of justice is felt deeply by the people he left behind.

BLOOD-STAINED

for Breonna Taylor and other Black women violated for "Associations while Black"

It was after hours when we finally succumb to
fatigue on a crisp Kentucky night.
Nebulous shadows swathed the room, we could scarcely see our silhouettes
if weren't for the luminous moon peeking through
the curtains and the lone streetlight
raking the weight of us and complementing a quiet
without the portent of the terrors that beset.

Lying sweetly in our love embrace, deep in a soothing slumber,
we were startled from a gentle dream, awakened by an ominous thunder
from the pounding at the door, and I wondered, 'whomever could that be for?'
"Who is there? What do you want?" I repeatedly implored.

My inquiry was met with a battering ram charging through the front.
I worked the frontlines all day; still, three guerillas
stood before me with heavy artillery.
Their trio and our pair studying the other and
preparing for an imminent affront
that commenced with a barrage of ammunition and
concluded with my punctured arteries.

Wait, I think the story of my death deserves a little more context.
My breaths are ragged now, I only have a few moments left:

D.B. MAYS

** We fired a warning shot first, they were plain clothed, we didn't know
It was the middle of night – we were startled
when they rammed in the front door.
They did not announce their authority, and I called out to them repeatedly.
In response to our single shot, they fired 32 times.
Why did they shoot so many when it only takes one to end someone's life?
Later, they said they were acting on a warrant for
alleged packages that I never received.
Even the USPS refuted these claims that LMPD made about me.
In fact, LMPD didn't conduct a search that night; they never looked for a thing.
Two months after killing me, they tried to disparage my memory,
pressuring a former love to implicate me in a drug trafficking ring. **

Must return to the scene because I feel my life slipping away from me;
I can't hold on any longer, I really can't ... I can't breathe.
Suspended before my carcass, I witnessed my bloodstained demise
and mourned my own loss as the tears spilled from my love's eyes.
Six minutes, no medics, I gasped as ragged breaths escaped my lungs.
"Hold on, Bre, hold on," my love pleaded, but I was already gone.

I drowned in my own life's blood as I heard my love weep for me.
Lord, wake us from this nightmare – we want to go back to sleep.

#SayHerName

for Black women and girls violated and killed by
police for "Being a Female while Black"

#SayHerName, but do not start or stop with the
police killing of #SandraBland in 2015.
While her death highlighted the susceptibility
of Black females to police brutality,
racial violence against Black women and girls has
persisted every century in American History.
Black females are subjected to unlawful detainment,
strip searches, rapes, and beatings.
In fact, sexual and physical abuse perpetrated by
persons who have legal authority
happen to Black women more frequently, violently,
and fatally than any other ethnicity.
Incidents against Black women and girls outnumber
white females by five to one,
and many Black women, like #Breonna and #Alteria,
are killed at home and unarmed.
When a female subject is Black, studies show that
police use of force increases rapidly,
and, too often, officers say that Black women and
girls are shot and killed *accidentally*,
meaning they were *combative* or *caught in crossfire*,
making them *collateral casualties.*

D.B. MAYS

The data underscore the vulnerability of Black
men and women to police brutality.
Black females account for 20 percent of the women
and girls fatally shot in this nation;
yet, Black women and girls are only 13 percent of the female population.
While Black men and boys make up 36 percent of
males who are shot lethally by police,
Black males are only 12 percent of the total male population of this country.
Pray tell, the homicides of Black women and girls
don't hike the media ratings or sales;
therefore, Black females killed by police receive
less media coverage than Black males.
Through these lines and verses, may their individual names and stories prevail,
may Black women and girls who have been
victimized by blue lives be memorialized,
and may thoughtful, honest discourse ensue about
police brutality and their tragic demise.

#SayHerName: LaVena Johnson was killed in her tent, not killed in action.
Only eight weeks after this five-foot-one, 20-year-
old soldier was deployed to Iraq,
evidence indicates that she was tortured and murdered in action while Black.
She was *assaulted and raped*, but *her death was ruled*
a suicide by the Department of Defense.
Her *broken nose, black eye, loose teeth,* and *chemical*
burns do not seem to be *self-inflicted*.
If DOD administrators had higher levels of
Emotional and Social Intelligence, or ESI,
they would not insult her family, community, and
nation with claims that she died by suicide.

#SayHerName: These women were imperfect, but they did not deserve to die.
Criminalized for traffic tickets, car crashes and chases,
summarily *justifying* their tragic demise.
Alexia Christian *shot herself while* she was *handcuffed*
and sitting in the backseat of a squad car.

Sharmel Edwards and Korryn Gaines were *massacred*
by police in questionable standoffs.
Mya Hall was *shot to death after mistakenly crashing*
her car into the gates of the NSA.
Miriam Carey was *gunned down after making a*
wrong turn at the White House gates.
Gabriella Navarez, Shantel Davis, and Melissa Williams
were *shot down in a high-speed chase.*
In every case, the system justified the officers'
excessive use of force and homicidal acts.
With higher ESI, police could've effectively de-escalated
and navigated a more humane track
that wouldn't've ended with the deaths of these
women for driving erratically while Black.

#SayHerName: These women were imperfect, but they did not deserve to die,
They were criminalized for mental illnesses,
summarily *justifying* their tragic demise.
The police *slammed* Tanisha Anderson *to death* on
the cold concrete in front of her family,
killed Michelle Cusseaux after she would *not comply*
be taken to a mental health facility,
shot Pearlie Golden *multiple times* for allegedly
wielding her gun, and *she was 93,*
suffocated Kayla Moore and Shereese Francis *to*
death for what police called *being EDP,*
an Emotionally Disturbed Person, not women who
needed help for their psychiatric disability.
In every case, the system justified the officers'
excessive use of force and homicidal acts.
With higher ESI, police could've effectively de-escalated
and navigated a more humane track
that wouldn't've ended with the murder of women
for living with a mental illness while Black.

#SayHerName: These women were imperfect, but they did not deserve to die.
They were criminalized for minor offenses,
summarily *justifying* their tragic demise.
Officers *hooded, shackled,* and *tasered* Natasha McKenna,
although she was mentally unwell.
Sheneque Proctor, 18 and arrested for disorderly
conduct, died *without explanation* in her cell.
Police *ignored* Kyam Livingston's *complaints of
pain* and her *repeated cries for help.*
Sandra Bland, arrested for a traffic violation, was
alone in her cell when she *killed herself.*
In every case, the system justified the officers'
excessive use of force and homicidal acts.
With higher ESI, police could've effectively de-escalated
and navigated a more humane track
that wouldn't've ended with the killing of women
and girls who were in-custody while Black.

#SayHerName: These women were imperfect, but they did not deserve to die.
They were criminalized for their associations,
summarily *justifying* their tragic demise.
Breonna Taylor was *murdered* after being *targeted
for a relationship* that had long ended.
Rekia Boyd was *shot in the head* by an officer who
felt disrespected by her and her friends.
Aiyana Jones was *killed during a midnight raid* led
police *to apprehend her aunt's boyfriend.*
In every case, the system justified the officers'
excessive use of force and homicidal acts.
With higher ESI, police could've effectively de-escalated
and navigated a more humane track
that wouldn't've ended with the homicides of women
and girls for associations while Black.

#SayHerName: These women were imperfect, but they did not deserve to die.
They were criminalized for domestic disputes,
summarily *justifying* their tragic demise.
Meagan Hockaday, Janisha Fonville, Aura Rosser
were *shot dead* for *allegedly wielding knives,*
Kanisha Necole Fuller was *shot in the head* for *being*
the love interest in the officer's lover's life.
Yvette Smith was *killed after calling* the police *for help*
to dissolve a dispute between two men.
Her deadly misstep was opening the door for police
and her crime, being a good friend.
In every case, the system justified the officers'
excessive use of force and homicidal acts.
With higher ESI, police could've effectively de-escalated
and navigated a more humane track
that wouldn't've ended with the killing of women for
being in domestic disputes while Black.

In most cases, the officers were cleared of all charges;
the blame was placed on the deceased.
Many officers still work and were later promoted
in their PDs for their valor and bravery.
While some civil settlements were made to make
problems go away, money can't buy lives,
daughters, mothers, or wives, or disguise that these
women and girls were victimized twice –
in life and death, while the people protest, and the
government denies and stands idly by.

BE THE LIGHT

for Black people who are "Tired of Being Tired while Black"

There is light at the end
of this long, winding path.
It may be so faint,
that it is too difficult to see it.
When we cannot find light,
we must create it and be it
for our progenies, legacies,
and generations to come.
Like our ancestors,
we must shine in the aftermath
and not succumb
to the darkness
but scatter our light
until the dust particles pass.
For our current is so strong,
discharge light at high frequency.
It's our nature to radiate high energy.
We ride beams of light,
we are light waves
following the vibrating path
that our elders paved.

We ride beams of light,
we are light waves
following the vibrating path
that our elders paved.

There is much power
in you and me
illuminating our light
collectively.
We must spark
a new way of thinking,
combine our wave crests
to form bright bands
and deftly navigate our way
through these dark lands.
We, who have infrared vision,
must reach out to guide
our brothers and sisters
who lack visibility,
to help them see their way
through the density
of dark space
that systems create
to keep us wandering,
for centuries,
through the abyss.
But, oh, we are the light,
we see through this!

Let us be the light that matters,
refracting as we pass through
corrupt institutions and agencies,
changing and dismantling
until they work in favor of me and you.

D.B. MAYS

Let us be the light that matters,
combusting to burn down
unjust systems and give shape
to new societal, economic,
educational, and judicial structures.
Let our light to be disruptive.

Spreading in all directions
our light is dispersed,
leaving a rainbow of Black
on this earth.

PART III

BLACK LINES

Black Bars and Beats #FortheCulture

STREET POLITICS: SQUAD UP

for the Black Panthers, The Squad, Stacey Abrams, 2020-2021 Mayors of Atlanta,
Baltimore, & D.C., Keiajah Brooks, Gary Chambers, Jr., Jemele Hill, Shaun King,
Tamika Mallory, Tangela Sears, and all Black activists who are leading efforts to
promote economic, social, and political reform for Black people. I couldn't name you
all, but to "Those Who Ride the Night Winds," #respect and keep #ridin!
Very loosely inspired by Talib Kweli's "Get By"

21st century, we woke up
Feelin fed up, we spoke up
They dissin us, they killin us
We got reasons, it's our season
Gotta give em, gotta give em, gotta give em,
Somethin to believe in
So, we leadin, yup, we leadin, we leadin

We so dope, we givin hope
Out in these streets getting these votes
Takin all the political heat
We makin changes for our peeps

Just gotta get votes, gotta get, gotta get VOTES!
Just gotta give hope, gotta give, gotta give HOPE!

Gotta give em, gotta give em, gotta give em,
Somethin to believe in
So, we leadin, yup, we leadin, we leadin ...

We squad up, bring political heat, reps go hard, cuz we got love fa da streets
Motivatin people to vote, get em to da box, got em movin they feet
Ain't career politicians, but da people from all hoods movin and listenin
Incumbents didn't see us comin, so we slide in, wasn't payin attention
Numbers roll in, Blitzer, Tapper, and King was on the hour

D.B. MAYS

Reportin how we beat em by margins, unseatin the centers of power
Yep, we in the primaries, makin big upsets, Dem and GOP primary defeats
Unprecedented moves, POC makin history, and we #SquadUp in victory

Outspent 18 to 1, but AOC closed Crowley's book like the Brook Avenue Press
Later, a Bowman *triumph* over Engel cuz da old Dems didn't *protect ya neck*
In a surprise victory, Pressley defeated Capuano, pushin for prison reform
Tliab ran unopposed, showed up and showed
out on the Hill, Arab dress, thobe on
Ilhan, a naturalized citizen but had landslide wins,
'18 and '20, swearin on the *Quran*
One of the first Muslim reps, and she stepped up on the Hill with her hijab on
In '20, Bush, in Missouri, upset Lacy Clay, ending a 52-year reign
Da streets sent a loud message, they wanted change, not more of the same

We on our political activism, good trouble, pressin political necks
They stay stressed, cuz we be keepin the balance in check
Ain't even move in good, but we gettin right down to business
on them riots on the Hill, introducin resolutions, COUPs, and commissions
For the *white supremacist insurrection*, the Squad wanted Trump impeached
Like Bush said, incited by POTUS, *the white supremacist-in-chief*
Squad hotter than six shades of hell, madder than a Texas trucker
*We're gonna go in there, and we're going to impeach the motherf****r!*

Tellin us, "Go back to your country!" Cuz sis rockin Senegalese twists,
and ain't nobody ever rep the Bronx from Puerto Rico like this?
Cuz she got the hijab on? Rockin a thobe? Askin if we American enough
Pish, tried to get at us on the Hill, but we're so damn American, stood up
and said, "You want that heat, we got that heat, cuz we built Ford tough!"

Keep comin fa da Squad, you gonna get that citizen relief
We on that Constitution-Rules-Everything-Around-Me, *C.R.E.A.M*
And that's on everything-we-touch-under-the-U.S.-sun belongs to WE
As long as the people rockin with the squad that's all we need

---

People said they need somethin to believe in, someone to lead them
The Squad bringin hope, no, bringin results that please them
We the lawmakers, call us people of color,
POC, squad reps all races, genders, and colors
We ya *dreamers and doers* and *immigrants,* too
We ya sisters and brothers, and we ridin for you

Don't fit the gang or the caucus, so establishment ain't feelin us
Threatened, they *try to discredit influencers,* call us disruptive
But that's okay, we came to cause a political raucous
Need some new blood, too many old bloodz corrupted
Like the Black Panthers, they say we radical, now we mainstream
If ya don't know, now you know, betta get on our team

We da young political gen, bringin old headz down if they don't let us in
Crippin all the way to the Hill, breakin glass ceilings, knockin doors in,
Turnin the system upside down, cuz dem old cats been trippin
They too busy politickin with lobbyists, we doin the heavy liftin
All under 50, we two decades younger than the majority reps
Average age, 38, they say we progressive cuz we go so left
On that tuition-free schools, no ICE, cancelin student debt
On that police reform, Green New Deal, and we gonna get, get get it
So, don't come for us, we social media savvy, we go heavy
Be sendin receipts all day, our Twitter fingaz stay ready

Just ask Ted Cruz, we got time today,
He'll tell you all about how shuckin and lyin don't pay
He all hat and no cattle, fake Texas longhorn, wasn't bred for battle
Drought got high, Cruz grabbed the first thang
smokin, hopped on a horse with no saddle
That's okay, when you abandon yo' state like a deadbeat daddy
We raise money for ya people, get em heat, food to eat, on our AOC
We know how ya voters feel, they got pocketbook problems
Go behind the bar, will ya? Get cha 2 mill in a day. Got problems? We solve em
But we operatin out a paper grocery bag, so we gone deliver it in cash,

Ready and rarin to go from da East, be there will
soon, sure'nuff, talkin Texas fast
Better Texas hold em, tell him to steer clear of da squad, different breed
We from the House, we squad up, we that what-in-
the-blue-blazes in Congressional country

21st century, we woke up
Feelin fed up, we spoke up
They dissin us, they killin us
We got reasons, it's our season
Gotta give em, gotta give em, gotta give em,
Somethin to believe in
So, we leadin, yup, we leadin, we leadin

We so dope, we givin hope
Out in these streets getting these votes
Takin all the political heat
We makin changes for our peeps

Just gotta get votes, gotta get, gotta get VOTES!
Just gotta give hope, gotta give, gotta give HOPE!

Gotta give em, gotta give em, gotta give em,
Somethin to believe in
So, we leadin, yup, we leadin, we leadin ...

We squad up from the Hill to states to the streetz
squad includes any person committed to justice and equity
People puttin their whole lives and everything on the line
for the protection of their community, including Black lives
Like these community leaders who be on the frontlines
Creatin spaces for the underrepresented but rarely gettin any shine
Street activists who demandin change and fightin injustice
Gettin death threats, names in fake news cuz they bein disruptive

Like Keiajah Brooks, Gen Z, a Justice Watcher, be confrontin Kentucky police
Gary Chambers, Jr., in Baton Rouge, readin the board
from A to Z about Robert E. Lee
Down in Miami, Tangela Sears been representin da streets, two decades long
Anti-violence activist, lost her son, David,
to a shooting, but she still goin strong
Workin for shooting victims and advocatin for public safety and racial equity
She from da 305, she ain't da one, don't come incorrect in her community
Get with Shaun King, he makes things happen,
takes all the hits for Black justice, man
Be givin the breakdown, he on the real,
stay guidin with the *North Star*, understand?
Tamika Mallory ain't askin for respect,
puttin systems in check, and makin demands
Been puttin in work before da Women's March
in '17, but you don't know NAN

Da streets respect Jemele Hill, cut from Sports Center, ESPN, for keepin it real,
Said fans should boycott the Dallas Cowboys for benchin players who kneel
Called POTUS a white supremacist, sayin what most of da country now feels
Hill was on the right side of history, the wrong
time, too early, so she got a raw deal

Baltimore Mayor, Brandon Scott be rockin his fro, workin for racial equity
Since 27, on police reform and public safety, gettin it in on dem Bmore streets,
Gives it straight, no ICE, ATL Mayor Keisha Lance Bottoms is bout that life
Like da FAMU Marching 100, she goes toe to toe with govz and prez,
no games, halftime
Up in DC, Browser on Muriel, paintin Black
Lives Matter all the way down 1600
That was a big boss move, Madam Mayor, youse a bad chick, just keepin it 100
Down in the dirty, Stacy Abrams, the real MVP, loss the governor's race in GA,
But she took that lost like a champ, gettin big Georgia wins,
flipped the whole damn state

#BlackLivesMatter originators, Alicia Garza, Patrisse Cullors, and Opal Tometi
Gave a call to action in '13, after Trayvon,
against racial violence and police brutality
Nothin has transformed street politics like Black Lives Matter
Showed us how to #SquadUp against oppression, now there's 40 BLM chapters
Advocatin for policy changes on race and Black liberation in all nations
A network of activists, anyone can fight for their community's self-preservation
So, to all the street activists and community organizers out here reppin for us
You an honorary squad member, fightin *against racism, oppression, injustice*

Yeah, call us apocalyptic, we bringin corrupt gov to an end
And we gonna stay in office, and in the streets, cuz *bullies don't win*
Yep, let the ole headz and good ole boyz know, we ain't comin to play
We on our Squad goals, we #SquadUp, we the Squad all day

Been puttin in work like the slave revolts, 1ˢᵗ century BC
Goin East African, like the Zanj, 869 AD
for 15 years from revolt to revolution in the Middle East
Desire for liberty so strong, we go Stono in the 13 colonies
Leadin us to independence like Toussaint led em in Haiti
Or Jamaica's Baptist War, from protest to rebellion, Samuel Sharpe, preach!
Risin up like enslaved Angolans, marchin da streets, chantin, *lukango,* Liberty!

"The squad includes any person committed to creating a more equitable and just world."
        "I can't name a single issue with roots in race that doesn't have economic implications, and I cannot think of a single economic issue that doesn't have racial implications. The idea that we have to separate them out and choose one is a con."
                                    – Alex Ocasio-Cortez, The Squad, Class of 2018,
                                            inaugural member, Bronx, NY

"I would say — our country should be more fearful of white men across our country, because they are actually causing most of the deaths within this country. And so, if

---

fear was the driving force of policies to keep America safe, Americans safe inside of this country, we should be profiling, monitoring, and creating policies to fight the radicalization of white men."

– Ilhan Abdullahi Omar, The Squad, Class of 2018, inaugural member, MN

"Represented here today are dreamers and doers, immigrants, people of every race identity, every gender identity and sexuality, sisters rocking Senegalese twists and hijabs."

"Don't let up, send emails, make phone calls … the reality is that there will be unrest in the streets for as long as there is unrest in our lives."

– Ayanna Pressley, The Squad, Class of 2018, inaugural member, MA

"We know what it feels like to be dehumanized, we know what it feels like to be brown and black in this country."

"And when your son looks at you and says,' Mama look, you won. Bullies don't win,' and I said,' Baby, they don't,' because United We're go na go in there and United We're going to impeach the motherf **** r."

– Rashida Harbi Tlaib, The Squad, Class of 2018, inaugural member, MI

"We have to stare White nationalism in the face, we have to deal with it directly, not only through law enforcement, but by recognizing that White nationalism lives in every American institution."

Jamal Bowman, The Squad, Class of 2020, NY

"Madam Speaker, St. Louis and I rise in support of the article of impeachment against Donald J. Trump. If we fail to remove a white supremacist president who incited a white supremacist insurrection, it's communities like Missouri's First District that suffer the most. The 117th Congress must understand that we have a mandate to legislate in defense of Black lives. The first step in that process is to root out white supremacy, starting with impeaching the white supremacist in chief."

Cori Bush, The Squad, Class of 2020, MO

"I'm not asking y'all for anything because y'all can't and won't be both my savior and my oppressor. I don't want reform. I want to turn this building into luxury low-cost housing. These would make some really nice apartments."

– Keiajah Brooks, Kansas City Black Lives Matter
Movement, Chingona Collective

D.B. MAYS

"This the most solidarity I done seen out of y'all in forever. Let's stand on this moving forward."

"If we come together around a shared vision for progress we will win."

— Gary Chambers, Jr., Baton Rouge Activist, Louisiana
U.S. House Congressional Candidate

"We want to see more work done by the city to stop this type of policing. We are tired of burying our black sons, brothers, nephews, and fathers at the hands of City of Miami cops." (2011)

"I knew that I was able to assist in making some things different, but I didn't understand the entire impact until I lost my son. When I sat with families, many didn't understand the process or understand how things should be done. ... I am an advocate in my community. I go to court with families."

— Tangela Sears, Political Consultant, Community
Activist, Parents of Murdered Children

"We are living in tumultuous times, and our focus should be fighting against the oppression and injustices that are against us - not battling those who are on the same side of seeking justice and peace."

"Young people, throughout history, have always been the lifeblood of every movement for civil and human rights."

— Shaun King, Activist, Writer, Real Justice PAC, The Breakdown, *North Star*

"We're not asking and begging for respect; we're demanding it."

"America has looted Black people! America looted the Native Americans when they first came here, so looting is what you do. We learned it from you. We learned violence from you! So, if you want us to do better, then damn it, you do better!"

"Young people...are enraged. And there's an easy way to stop it. Arrest the cops. Charge the cops. Charge all the cops. Not just some of them. Not just here in Minneapolis. Charge them in every city across America where our people are being murdered."

— Tamika Mallory, Activist, Writer, NBMBA, former
National Chair of Women's March

THIS IS WRONG

*for any Black person who has ever experienced any of
this. Inspired by Tupac's "Life Goes On"*

How many Blacks been killed by police?
What do we have to do to get justice in these streets?
We're at war, they keep killin you and me
They say this is the way it is, but this is wrong
How many Blacks been killed by police?
What do we have to get justice in these streets?
We're at war, they keep killin you and me
They say this is the way it is, but this is wrong

They get on the TV to tell us what we see
The video was clear, we know what's happening
They choked you out, left you dying in the street
Took everybody down who filmed them at the scene
Went through your posts, show you flashin ya grill
Now youse a gang banger who was ready to kill
Makin you a criminal in death, wasn't one in life
You ain't never did crime, ain't never did time
Can't really do justice to ya memory in this rhyme
We all strugglin to get through
But we too busy, defending you in interviews
Court of public opinion convict you, posthumously
Family can't grieve ... properly
We waitin on justice, but they don't give a damn
We hashtag ya name, post ya pics on the Gram
Nobody cares when it's us, we get no love ... we thugs
This is wrong

How many Blacks been killed by police?
What do we have to do to get justice in these streets?
We're at war, they keep killin you and me
They say this is the way it is, but this is wrong
How many Blacks been killed by police?
What do we have to get justice in these streets?
We're at war, they keep killin you and me
They say this is the way it is, but this is wrong

Yeah, bruh, we know the judge gave you life
Don't care what they say, this here ain't right
No criminal history, but the sentencing
Based on false testimonies ... minimum mandatories
No plea deal, the lawyer workin for the other side
Comin back to you, tellin ya nothin but lies
By the time it's over, know you ain't comin home
Had to put it all in a song, cuz this is wrong
Holdin ya kids down, put that on everything
Til you free, keep money on ya commissary
Don't let the time do you, bruh, you do the time
Keep ya hands in prayers and head to the sky
We stand tall, but the tears fall from our eyes
Sendin prayers up for you every night
Until yo delivery
Hold ya head up, JD
This is wrong

How many Blacks been killed by police?
What do we have to do to get justice in these streets?
We're at war, they keep killin you and me
They say this is the way it is, but this is wrong
How many Blacks been killed by police?
What do we have to get justice in these streets?
We're at war, they keep killin you and me
They say this is the way it is, but this is wrong

My phone rings, check my ID, and I see it's you
Say the police trailin you, askin me what to do
I tell you to drive slow since you're almost home
I hop in the car, meet you out on the road
Cuz I ain't gonna let you do this all alone
Pull into the driveway, the last to pull in, my car
I tell you to stay inside yours, film from afar
The cop is upset, yells at us both to "Get out!"
Lights flashin bright, sirens blarin loud
I ask him what is this all about,
Why did he need to trail us to our house?
No answer, draws his gun, points it your way
Nah, not today. I intercept, take a hit to the face
My blood oozing, spilling all over the place,
The last thing I hear is you scream, "Mommy!"
Traumatized by what you're witnessing
But, baby, it was you or me
This is wrong

BLACK LOVE

for Black couples who inspire us with their flavor of # BlackLove

Let's raise a glass to #BlackLove
Round of applause for #BlackLove
On that you're all I need to get by, #BlackLove
That melanin magic, #Black Love
Make it happen, #Black Love
Nothing even matters, #BlackLove
LoveHappy, Hood Love, Good Love #BlackLove
That it's whateva, together forever, #BlackLove

Want that type of #BlackLove, made for music and TV
Post bout it on the gram, hashtag it in Tweets
The kind of #BlackLove creatin Black legacies
#BlackOnBlack couples buildin Black dynasties
We on that type of #BlackLove, baby, you and me
We *conceited*, please believe it, big *egos* and things
Team paperchase, yeah, we goin *all the way up*
and every day, we celebrate, raisin gold-rimmed cups

Need a shot of Remy – nah, pour me a glass of Papoose
If you hold me down for seven, yeah, I'm marrying you
I'm your Keisha, cop me Gucci, gonna flip us a grip
Blend families, a trap dynasty like Tiny and Tip
Be ya around the way girl, Smithin it, Simone and LL
Gettin it in since 95, and we still *rock the bells*
Be gangsta media moguls, '92, like Kim and Ice Cube
Raisin brows on Fridays, today is a good day, you know how we do

---

Let's get married to hip hop, like Rev Run and Justine
Walk this way in *my Adidas*, if you know what I mean
On that Snoop and Shante, we learned to lay low
squinty eyed on love's highs and lows, but that's how #BlackLove goes
You gift me 12 days of Christmas and a fly family
Rock couture fits on vacays like Casey and DJ Envy
Like this, Kelly Rowland and Tim, be my *motivation* like him, ya know
Lay it on me all night, like I stole sumthin, puttin them *kisses down low*
We a Legend, like Christy Tiegen, postin "Dear John" tweets,
You hit me back with emojis when ya sittin right next to me

Let's raise a glass to #BlackLove
Round of applause for #BlackLove
On that you're all I need to get by, #BlackLove
That melanin magic, #Black Love
Make it happen, #Black Love
Nothing even matters, #BlackLove
LoveHappy, Hood Love, Good Love #BlackLove
That it's whateva, together forever, #BlackLove

On my Lady London, marathon runnin, holdin Nip down
On our Hussle, you the Nipsey to my pretty brown, brown
Like 2 Chainz, Kesha Ward, *we own it*, our love, *it's a vibe*
I'm the Keys to ya Beatz, bruh, *love looks better* on 'dis side
Naw, I'm trippin, but for real, got an *empire state of mind*
A *million ways to get it* for these *Bills, Bills, Bills*; so, together we shine
Like Kandi Burruss ... Todd Tucker, I'm queenin, and you playin the post
On our Faith and Biggie, uhm, Faith and Stevie J, we be doin the most

Like Fabolous and Emmy B, we be wilin, but keep our beef out the streets
It's a *lituation*, just *can't let you go, baby*, you know how it be
Chasin' Bacardi with Offset, *YRN*-stressed, but I'm still takin you back
Because I don't care what they say, it's sumthin bout that Black on Black.
We *lovehappy*, but thinkin on the things we do gives me *Déjà vu*
I'm *drunk in love*; so, don't get ya neck checked in our *family feud*
Yeah, we on our Jay and B, but don't Becky me; that was publicity, get me?

On the real, who else we gone follow on this *Black effect*, feel me?
On the run since the 90's, we *crazy in love*, everybody *heard about us*,
But everything is everything, yuh, when we on that ... #BlackLove

Let's raise a glass to #BlackLove
Round of applause for #BlackLove
On that you're all I need to get by, #BlackLove
That melanin magic, #Black Love
Make it happen, #Black Love
Nothing even matters, #BlackLove
LoveHappy, Hood Love, Good Love #BlackLove
That it's whateva, together forever, #BlackLove

We the Johnsons, ya Cookie to *Black Magic*, collectin companies and rings
Savannah holdin ya south end, since rookie year, now we doin King things
On that Tamia and Grant Hill, *into you, loving you still*, 20 years in
The Steph to my Ayesha, everyting irie when ya curry attention,
QB to my Ciara, Russ, *level me up*! In football, family, and God we trust
Be Kijafa to Mike Vick, stay in the end zone; why they worryin bout us?
On our Westbrook, Nina and Russell, MVPs ... we Bruins, both of us ball
Now, we at Wake Forest fallin in Black college love like Jada and Chris Paul

Shepherd a Black family, Sterling and Iman, we keep it pretty and brown,
Rockin Chanel all day, all night, I'm that model wife, holdin it down
Co-starrin Gabrielle and D-Wade, playin *Love and Basketball* in real life
Morissa and Malcom J, roots and *Freedom* rising where the Eagles fly high
How you want it, seductive, like Teyana and Shump? We in the 2-3 zone, it's on
Chocolate city like Morgan and Marquise G, we got a Black mecca at home
On our Tawanna and AI, called it a game, no crossovers, so, we back together
No substitutions, be Melo and LaLa, take a lot shots and miss, but it's whatever,
we gone be together forever!

Let's raise a glass to #BlackLove
Round of applause for #BlackLove
On that you're all I need to get by, #BlackLove
That melanin magic, #Black Love

Make it happen, #Black Love
Nothing even matters, #BlackLove
LoveHappy, Hood Love, Good Love #BlackLove
That it's whateva, together forever, #BlackLove

Big game, LaTanya and Samuel Jackson, *pulp fiction*, that's who we be
Fighting temptations, keeping the Black family together, revolutionaries
Beloved like Pauletta and Denzel, birthing a Black film dynasty
They see *American gangster*, but we see *glory*, writing our own story
Yes, *it's the little things* off screen, that's why *she's gotta have it*
He got game, but she's the *real MVP*, Black team, team Black, we savage
Be on that Tina and Matt Knowles raising destiny's child, buildin
We the Lawsons, we awesome - you got kids, I
got kids, now they *all my children*

Just the two of us, like Will and Jada, we *set if off* cuz *opposites attract*
Sometimes I *girls trip*, but don't act *nutty*, I gotta thing for *men in black*
We in the *matrix*, red or blue? Gettin some things
wrong, gettin most things right
Scream you leavin, got ya *John Hancock* on that doc, so, you my *bad boy* for life
Baby, ain't nothin better than *kissin you*, there's *no one else* cuz we *in too deep*
On our Omar and Keisha Epps, ever since we
got that *juice*, we been *major league*
Chesnut-colored couple, we on our Morris and Pam, fam –
We *not easily broken* because youse the *best man*
Like dem *boyz in the hood*, *breaking all the rules* cuz you was *under siege*
but you been *thinkin like a man*, the *perfect guy*, since you got with me

Get on ya Sterling K. Brown, and keep me in the *first wives club*
Yeah, *this is us*, I'll be Ryan Michelle Bathe, and keep it *all about us*
Black panther, givin me keys to the kingdom, we on that Wakanda forever
On our Boris Kodjoe and Nicole Parker, *code black*, we look good together
Keep it fresh with date nights and neck kisses, boyfriend, don't lose the spark
Addicted to that *brown sugar*, give her *soul food, whatever she wants,*
Even through tough times, on our Holly Robinson
and Rodney Peete, *like family*

Lettin you run game all night, but with the sunrise, it's *morning show mysteries*
Glad you made *contact*, been *waiting to exhale* and get my *groove back*, babe
You make *love easy*, you got a certain *state of mind*, got me *walking on blind faith*
That's why we *jumping the broom*, like Angela Baskett and
Courtney B., #BlackLove and Black ivy league
Now, we *soul panthers*, scaling *fences*, ain't gettin
ambushed in this *lovecraft country*.
We be Debbie Allen, Norm Nixon, since '84,
we courtin, we own the dance floor
Winnin everything from Emmys to NBA rings, but whose keepin score?
Too busy buildin for our legacy, we never *out-of-sync*, focus is primetime
We live in a *different world*, *fame* doesn't matter, so, we
writin *blank checks* cuz what's yours is mine

We on that wealth whispers, #relationshipgoals, like Winfrey and Graham
'86 all rumors, keep it on the low, cuz we ain't doin it for the gram
Be like Spike and Tonya Lee, we puttin everyone on, makin cinema history
Raisin *healthy babies* and Black consciousness through film and TV
Tacklin everything that affects Black – race, crime, poverty, and love
We be on that *Malcom X, ya dig?* By any means necessary, *sho nuff*
Never *bamboozled* cuz you the *inside man*, ya information on point
We producin a positive portrayal of our Black family like a *Spike Lee joint*
On our Ossie Davis and Ruby Dee, we *do the right thing*
We got that type of #BlackLove that's made for film and TV
We married to the struggle, right on, *for love of liberty*
Till death do us part, we *raisins in the sun*, stage left, exit scene

Let's raise a glass to #BlackLove
Round of applause for #BlackLove
On that you're all I need to get by, #BlackLove
That melanin magic, #Black Love
Make it happen, #Black Love
Nothing even matters, #BlackLove
LoveHappy, Hood Love, Good Love #BlackLove
That it's whateva, together forever, #BlackLove

Amy to Marcus Garvey, #BlackLove
Be your Myrlie to Medgar Evers, #BlackLove
Betty to Malcom X, #BlackLove
Coretta to Martin Luther King, #BlackLove
Akua to Fred Hampton, #BlackLove
Juanita to Ralph D. Abernathy, #BlackLove
Evelyn to Joseph Lowery, #BlackLove
Octavia to C.T. Vivian, #BlackLove
Jean to Andrew Young, #BlackLove
Be your Michelle to Barack, #BlackLove

ACKNOWLEDGEMENTS

For my beta reader review team, I can't express enough my gratitude for the tremendous effort you put into reading and reviewing this work. Your feedback was invaluable. You are the real MVPs! Thank you to Pinnacle Designs for creating the cover concept and to @Pandora_Halk Graphic Designer/Fiverr for your assistance with bringing the vision to life. I could not have pulled this off without the amazing work of my interior book formatter, @Richellb/Fiverr. Thank you! Thank you to my publisher, Pinnacle Performance Learning Group, LLC. for absolutely everything.

My completion of this project would not have been accomplished without the support of my family. Thank you for believing in me and for encouraging me to "stop posting on social media and to write a book about it!" I am grateful to my mother, siblings, and sister-in-law for being my sounding board early in the process and for not blocking my series of daily texts. I thank my children for critiquing my work and offering thoughtful reviews whenever I needed one.

Finally, I am especially thankful for my caring and supportive husband who was always a willing food delivery serviceman, bartender, and house manager when I needed him to be. Thank you for falling in love with my poetry along the way. I love and appreciate my family for the encouragement you all gave when I struggled. Thanks to all of you, I am published author now!

ABOUT THE AUTHOR

Black Lives, Lines, and Lyrics is the first book by D.B. Mays, a highly decorated urban educator who has spent over two decades working on the local and national levels to promote education equity and support the education and empowerment of students in underserved schools and communities. In addition to her own lived experiences with institutional racism, racial and social injustice, and education, housing, and healthcare inequities, the Black Lives Matter movement and the victims of racial violence inspired her to write this work. Her poetry collection explores a variety of themes ranging from Blackness, discrimination, life, loss, trauma, racial violence, and revolution. She is also the author of the forthcoming historical fiction series *The Tree of Anglee*. You can learn more on her website, www.authordbmays.com and her Facebook and Instagram pages @ authordbmays. A proud HBCU graduate and mother of two, she lives in Atlanta, Georgia with her husband.

COPYRIGHT PERMISSIONS

Every effort has been made to trace or contact all copyright holders. The publishers will be pleased to make good any omissions or rectify any mistakes brought to their attention at the earliest opportunity. For concerns, address: authordbmays@p2learninggroup.com.

REFERENCES

American Psychological Association. "Incarceration Nation: The United States Leads the World in Incarceration. A New Report Explores Why - And Offers Recommendations for Fixing the System." *American Psychological Association*, Vol 45, No. 9. American Psychological Association, Oct. 2014. Web.

Akili, Greg; Bargoma MD, Emilee. "Say Her Name: Dr. Susan Moore and Medical Apartheid." *The Root*. The Glow Up, 15 Jan. 21. Web.

Anderson, Jessica; Broadwater, Luke. "All Six Officers Charged in Freddie Gray's Death Released on Bail." The Baltimore Sun. Baltimore Sun, 3 May 2015. Web.

Andone, Dakin. "Elijah McClain Died after a Police Encounter almost One Year Ago. Here's What Happened Since." *CNN*. CNN, 24 Aug. 2020. Web.

Bailey, Holly. "Judge Dismisses Third-Degree Murder Charge against Officer in George Floyd's Death; Upholds More Serious Charge." *The Washington Post*. Washington Post, 22 Oct. 2020. Web.

Baker, Al; Goodman, J. David; Mueller, Benjamin. "Beyond the Chokehold: The Path to Eric Garner's Death." *The New York Times*. NY Times. 13 Jun. 2015. Web.

BBC Contributors. "Black Lives Matter Founders: We Fought to Change History and We Won." *BBC News*. BBC, 30 Nov. 2020. Web.

BBC Contributors. "Korryn Gaines shooting: US Police Kill Woman as Child Watched." *BBC News*. BBC, 2 Aug. 2016. Web.

BBC Contributors. "Tamir Rice: US Police Kill Boy, 12, Carrying Replica Gun." *BBC News*. BBC, 24 Nov. 2014. Web.

Bacon, John; Jervis, Rick. "Fort Worth police chief: 'No excuse' for Aaron Dean to shoot Atatiana Jefferson in her home." *USA Today*. USA Today, 18 Oct. 2019. Web.

Barajas, Joshua. "Freddie Gray's Death Ruled a Homicide." (video & text). *PBS*. PBS, 1 May 2015. Web.

Bever, Lindsey; Costa, Robert. "9 Dead in Shooting at Historic Charleston African American church. Police Chief Calls It 'Hate Crime.'" *The Washington Post*. Washington Post, 17 Jun. 2015. Web.

Blinder, Alan. "Ex-Officer Who Shot Walter Scott Pleads Guilty in Charleston." *The New York Times*. NY Times, 2 May 2017. Web.

Boroff, David. "Slager Gets 19 to 24 Years in Fatal Shooting of Walter Scott." *New York Daily News*. NY Daily News, 2 Dec. 2017. Web.

Botelho, Greg. "Officials Detail Sandra Bland Autopsy Findings." *CNN*. CNN, 23 Jul. 2015. Web.

Bowden, John. "Death of Andre Hill Ruled Homicide as Police Officer Awaits Employment Ruling." *The Hill*. The Hill, 28 Dec. 2020. Web.

Bruner, Bethany. "Here's Video and a Timeline of The Andre Hill Shooting by Columbus Police." *The Columbus Dispatch*. Dispatch. 23 Dec. 2020. Web.

Charles, Kerry. "Casey Goodson Jr. Shot Six Times by Deputy Jason Meade, Family Attorney Says Asey Goodson Jr. Shot Six Times by Deputy Jason Meade, Family Attorney Says." NBC4i. NBC4i, 10 Feb. 2021. Web.

Chuck, Elizabeth. "An amazing first step': Advocates hail Congress's maternal mortality prevention bill." *NBC News*. NBC News, 19 Dec. 2018. Web.

CNN Contributors. "Protests across the Globe after George Floyd's Death." CNN World. CNN 13 Jun. 2020. Web.

Coates, Ta-Nehisi. "The Life Breonna Taylor Lived, in the Words of Her Mother." *Vanity Fair*. Vanity Fair, 24 Aug. 2020. Web.

Condon, Bernard; Richmond, Todd. "Minneapolis Requires Cops to Stop Unreasonable Force, but Officers in George Floyd's Arrest didn't Intervene." *ABC 7*. Associated Press, 7 Jun. 2020. Web.

Czachor, Emily. "George Floyd Did Not Have a Pulse When Medics Placed Him in Ambulance, Minneapolis Fire Department Report Shows." Newsweek. Newsweek, 27 May 2020. Web.

Dator, James. "Naomi Osaka's Protests are a Lesson on Power and Bravery: Naomi is Protesting without The Support of a Team Behind Her." SB Nation, 3 Sept. 2020. Web.

Duret, Daphne. "Who Was Corey Jones? Life's Passions and Loves of A Man Shot and Killed by a Police Officer." Palm Beach Post. 30 Oct. 2015. Web.

Flynn, Sean. "How to Make a Police Shooting Disappear: The Tamir Rice Story." GQ. GQ, 10 Feb. 2021. Web.

Garel, Connor. "WNBA Players Protested Police Brutality Even Before Colin Kaepernick. Remember That?" *The Huffington Post*. Huffington Post, 8 Aug. 2020. Web.

Glawe, Justin, Net.al. "Rayshard Brooks police shooting was homicide, says medical examiner". *The Guardian*. The Guardian, 15 Jun. 2020. Web.

Hauser, Christine. "Florida University to Award Posthumous Degree to Trayvon Martin." *New York Times*. NY Times, 5 May 2017. Web.

Hutchinson, Bill. "Black Doctor Dies of COVID After Alleging Hospital Mistreatment: 'This is How Black People Get Killed.'" *ABC News*. ABC News, 24 Dec. 2020. Web.

Johnson, Jason. "Star-Spangled Bigotry: The Hidden Racist History of the National Anthem." *The Root*. The Root, 4 Jul. 2016. Web.

Johnson, Stephon. "Ramsey Orta in and out of solitary confinement, abused by officers." *New York Amsterdam News*. Amsterdam News, 2 Jan. 2020.

Johnson, Tahira. "Maternity Care in Crisis." State Legislatures. NCSL, Jan/Feb. 2019. Web.

Jordan, Sandra. "Documents and Photos Suggest Foul Play in Death of Private Johnson." *The St. Louis American*. STL American, 5 May 2014. Web.

Khaleeli, Homa. "#Sayhername: Why Kimberlé Crenshaw is Fighting for Forgotten Women." *The Guardian*. The Guardian, 30 May 2016. Web.

King, Akili. "Activist Tamika D. Mallory on Her Viral Speech and What True Allyship Looks Like." *Vogue*. Vogue. 6 Jun. 2020. Web.

King, Danae. "Ohio Deputy Who Killed Casey Goodson has Used Faith to Justify Use of Force Before." *The Columbus Dispatch*. USA Today, 29 Dec. 2020. Web.

King, Erica. "Widowed Father Works with Congresswoman on Legislation to Prevent Maternal Deaths." *ABC News*. ABC News, 6 Jun. 2019. Web.

Knapp, Andrew; Darlington, Abigail. "Dylann Roof's 9 Life Sentences on State Murder Charges 'Surest' Route to Federal Execution, Prosecutor Says." *Post & Courier*. Post and Courier, 10 Apr. 2017. Web.

LaFraniere, Sharon; Oppel Jr., Richard A.; Montgomery, David. "Texas County's Racial Past Is Seen as Prelude to Sandra Bland's Death". The New York Times. NY Times, 26 Jul. 2015. Web.

Lartey, Jamiles. "The 'Ali Summit': A Turning Point in Sports' Fight against Injustice." *The Guardian*, 23, Oct 2017. Web.

Linderman, Juliet. "The Latest: Facebook Suspended Account During Standoff." *Star Tribune*. Star Tribune, 3 Aug. 2016. Web.

McLaughlin, Eliott C.; Cooper, Aaron; Sanchez, Ray. "Freddie Gray verdict: Officer Edward Nero not guilty." *CNN*. CNN, 23 May 2016. Web.

Mustian, Jim; Deslatte, Melinda. "Ronald Greene's Family Views Graphic Video of His Death in Louisiana State Police Custody." *The Advocate*. The Advocate, 15 Oct. 2020. Web.

NAACP. "Criminal Justice Fact Sheet." National Association for the Advancement of Colored People. NAACP. Web.

NBC News Contributor. "Video Shows Cleveland Cop Shoot 12-Year-Old Tamir Rice Within Seconds." NBC News. NBC News, 26 Nov. 2014. Web.

Nolan, Emma. "Live PD' Destroyed Video of Texas Man Javier Ambler Saying: 'I Can't Breathe' Before Dying in Police Custody." *Newsweek*. Newsweek, 10 Jun. 2020. Web.

Ortiz, Erik. "Elijah McClain Was Injected with Ketamine while Handcuffed. Some Medical Experts Worry about its Use During Police Calls." *NBC News*. NBC News, 1 Jul. 2020. Web.

Plohetski, Tony. "Williamson County Sheriff Robert Chody indicted in Javier Ambler Case". *Austin American-Statesman*. Statesman, 7 Jan. 2021. Web.

Ramaswamy, Chitra. "Trayvon Martin's parents, five years on: 'Racism is alive and well in America.'" *The Guardian*. The Guardian, 13 Feb. 2017. Web.

Robles, Frances. "The Citizen's Arrest Law Cited in Arbery's Killing Dates Back to the Civil War." *The New York Times*. NY Times, 14 May 2020. Web.

Rogers, Katie. "Sandra Bland's Autopsy Details How She Died." *The New York Times*. NY Times, 25 Jul. 2015. Web.

Ross, Janell. "Ron Davis, Father of Slain Florida Teen Jordan Davis, Ready to Fight." *The Huffington Post*. The Huffington Post, 25 Jan. 2013. Web.

Rueb, Emily S. "Ex-Officer in Florida Gets 25 Years in Prison for Killing Black Man." *New York Times*. NY Times, 25 Apr. 2019. Web.

Savali, Kirsten West. "What Happened to Quawan Charles?" *Essence*. Essence, 11 Nov. 2020. Web.

Sawyer, Wendy. "Mass Incarceration: The Whole Pie 2020." Prison Policy Initiative, 24 Mar. 2020. Web.

Schlosberg, Jon; Yang, Allie. "'Suspicious' Circumstances around Black Teen Found Dead in Louisiana." *ABC News*. ABC News, 14 Nov. 2020. Web.

Shaffer, Corey. "Cleveland Police Officer Shoots 12-Year-Old Boy Carrying BB Gun." *Cleveland*. Cleveland, 12 Jan. 2019. Web.

Silver, Mark. *3 1/2 Minutes, 10 Bullets*. *Amazon Prime Video*. Amazon, 2015. Web.

Sullivan, Kate. "Here are the 4 Congresswomen known as 'The Squad' Targeted by Trump's Racist Tweets." *CNN Politics*. CNN, 16. Jul 2019. Web.

Wells MD, Lindsey; Gowda MD, Arjun. "A Legacy of Mistrust: African Americans and the US Healthcare System." Proceedings of UCLA Health, Vol. 24. UCLA Med, 2020. Web.

Wesley Lowery. "Plainclothes Officer Who Killed Florida Church Drummer is Charged with Manslaughter, Attempted Murder." *The Washington Post*. Washington, Post, 1 Jun. 2016. Web.

Wood, Pamela; Knezevich, Alison. "Jury Awards More than $37M to Family of Korryn Gaines in Civil Case against Baltimore County." *The Baltimore Sun*. Baltimore Sun, 16 Feb. 2018. Web.

Wikipedia contributors. "Killing of Aiyana Jones." Wikipedia, The Free Encyclopedia. Wikipedia, The Free Encyclopedia, 3 Feb. 2021. Web.

Wikipedia contributors. "Tamika Mallory." Wikipedia, The Free Encyclopedia. Wikipedia, The Free Encyclopedia, 3 Feb. 2021. Web.

Wikipedia contributors. "Shaun King." Wikipedia, The Free Encyclopedia. Wikipedia, The Free Encyclopedia, 3 Feb. 2021. Web.

Wikipedia contributors. "The Squad." *Wikipedia, The Free Encyclopedia*. Wikipedia, The Free Encyclopedia, 3 Feb. 2021. Web.

Williams Crenshaw Kimberlé; Ritchie, Andrea J.; Anspach, Rachel; Gilmer, Rachel; Harris, Luke. SHN: Resisting Police Brutality Against Black Women." The African American Policy Forum. AAPF, 2015. Web.

Wing, Nick. "A Grand Jury Did Indict One Person Involved in Eric Garner's Killing -- The Man Who Filmed It." *The Huffington Post*. The Huffington Post, 3 Dec. 2014. Web.

Made in the USA
Columbia, SC
14 March 2021

34461756R00136